A RUMOR IN ST. PETERSBURG

Words and Music by LYNN AHRENS
and STEPHEN FLAHERTY

Moderately, with motion

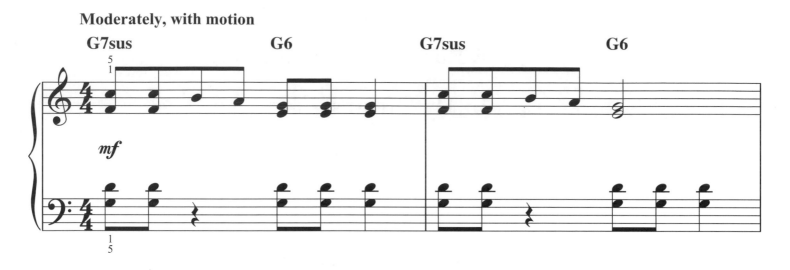

emp - ty pot. "A bright-er day is dawn- ing. It's al - most at hand!" The

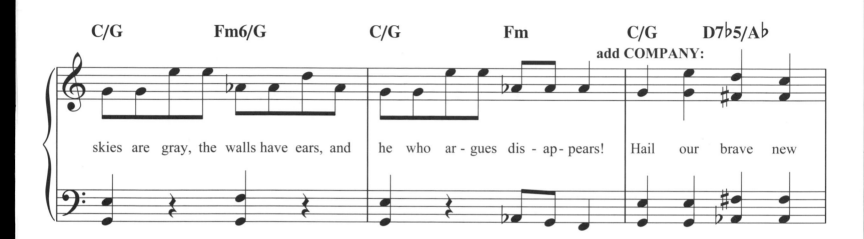

skies are gray, the walls have ears, and he who ar - gues dis - ap-pears! Hail our brave new

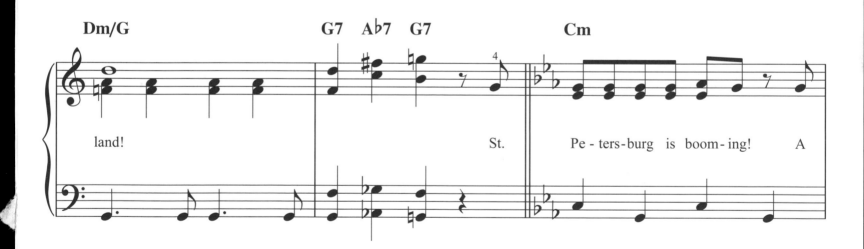

land! St. Pe -ters-burg is boom-ing! A

cit - y on the rise! It's real - ly ver - y friend-ly, if you don't mind spies! We

stand be-hind our lead-ers and stand in line for bread! We're good and loy - al com-rades and our

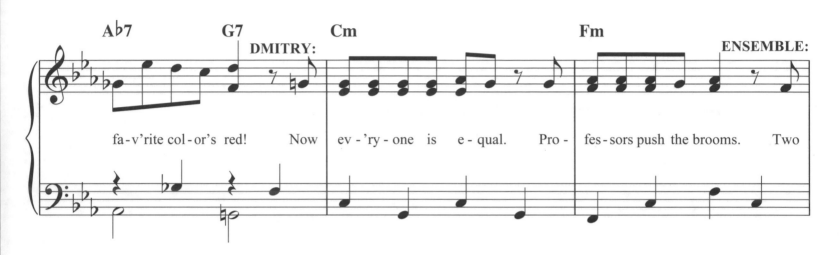

DMITRY: fa-v'rite col-or's red! Now ev-'ry-one is e-qual. Pro - fes-sors push the brooms. **ENSEMBLE:** Two

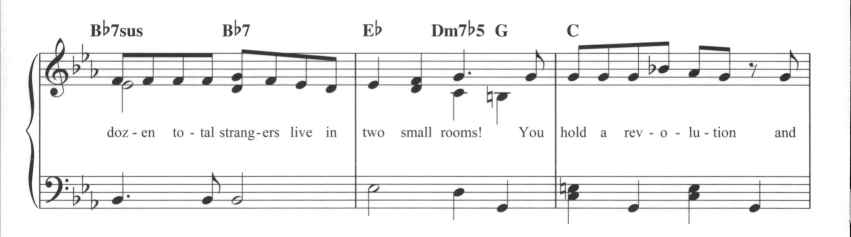

doz - en to - tal strang-ers live in two small rooms! You hold a rev - o - lu - tion and

here's the price you pay! Thank good - ness for the gos - sip! *Spa -*

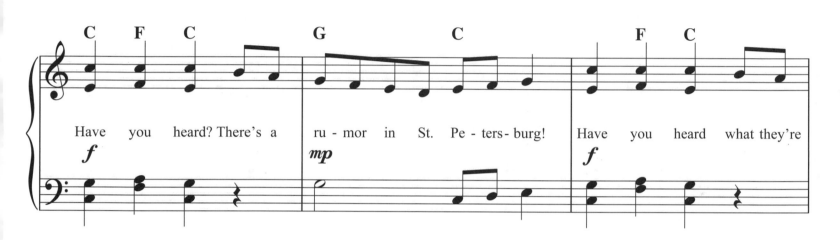

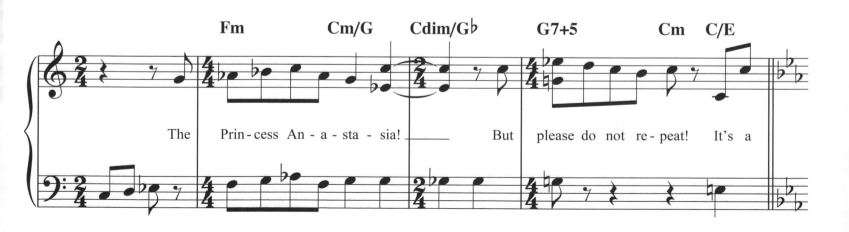

ru - mor, a leg- end, a mys- ter- y! Some-thing whis-pered in an al - ley-way or

through a crack! It's a ru - mor that's part of our his - to-ry! They

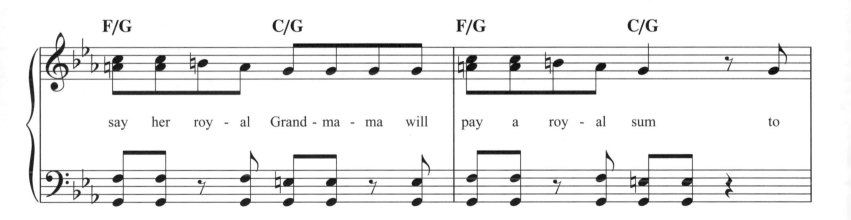

say her roy - al Grand-ma - ma will pay a roy - al sum to

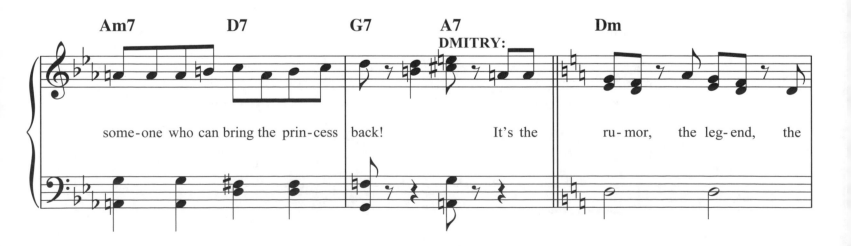

some-one who can bring the prin-cess back! It's the ru - mor, the leg- end, the

9

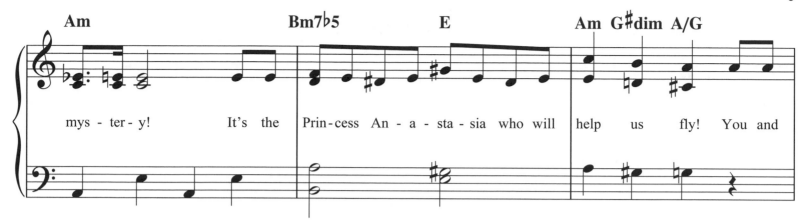

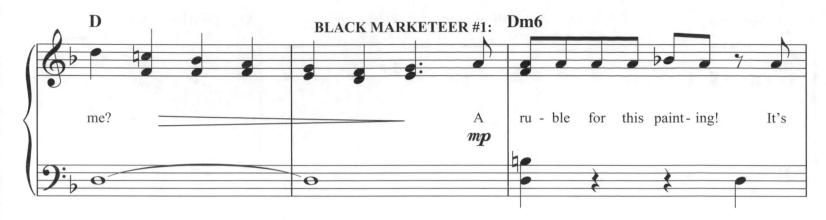

me?

BLACK MARKETEER #1:

A ru - ble for this paint - ing! It's

mp

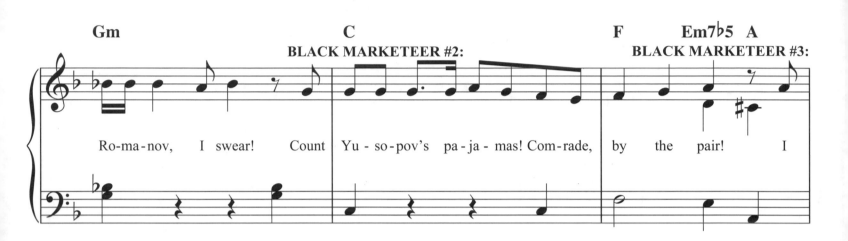

BLACK MARKETEER #2:

Ro - ma - nov, I swear! Count Yu - so - pov's pa - ja - mas! Com - rade, by the pair! I

BLACK MARKETEER #3:

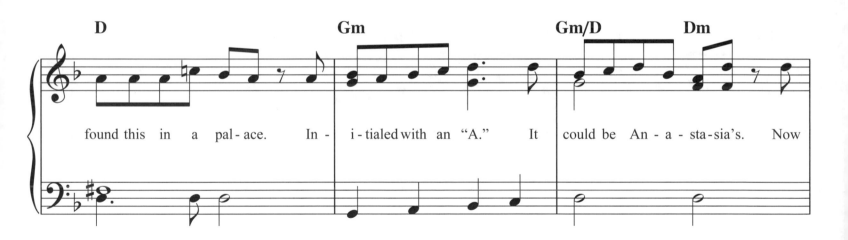

found this in a pal - ace. In - i - tialed with an "A." It could be An - a - sta - sia's. Now

DMITRY:

what will some - one pay? Now, it's risk - y but not more than u - su - al. We'll need

mf

pa - pers, we'll need tick - ets, we'll need nerves of steel! Yes, it's risk - y... a lot more than

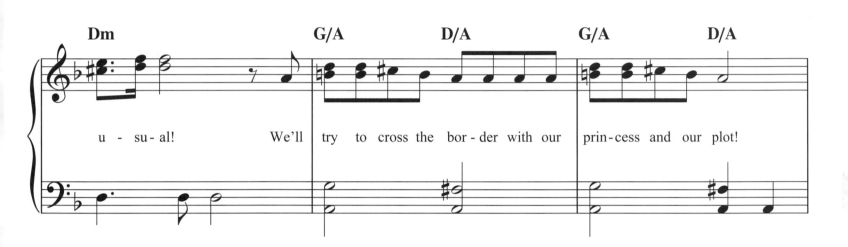

u - su - al! We'll try to cross the bor - der with our prin - cess and our plot!

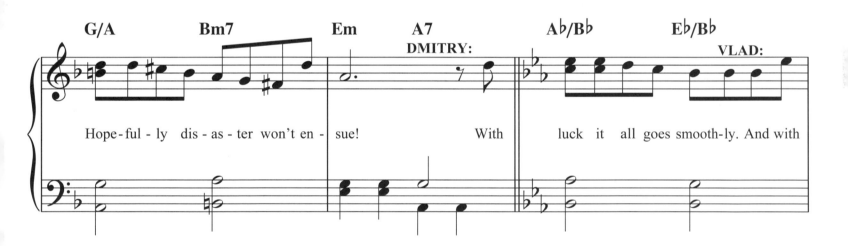

Hope - ful - ly dis - as - ter won't en - sue! With luck it all goes smooth - ly. And with

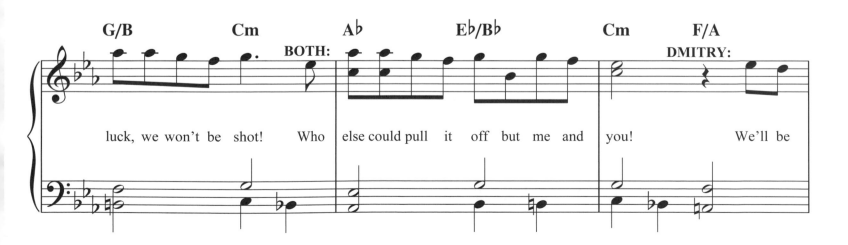

luck, we won't be shot! Who else could pull it off but me and you! We'll be

Eb/Bb   **Eb/B**   **Cm**   **Cm/Bb**   **F7/A**   **F7**

VLAD: DMITRY: VLAD: BOTH:

rich! We'll be rich! We'll be   out! We'll be out! And St.   Pe - ters-burg will have some more to

Bb7   ENSEMBLE:

talk a - bout!   I heard it from a per-son,   I heard it from a per-son who as-

mp

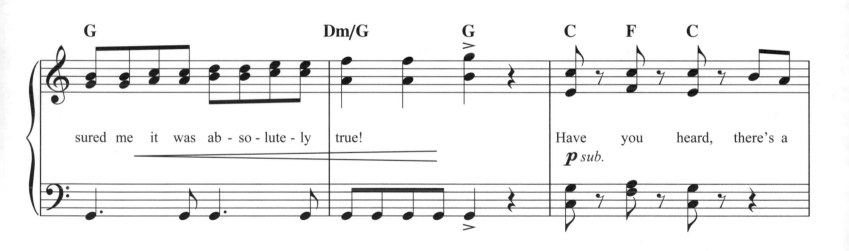

G   **Dm/G**   **G**   **C**   **F**   **C**

sured me it was ab - so - lute - ly true!   Have you heard, there's a

p sub.

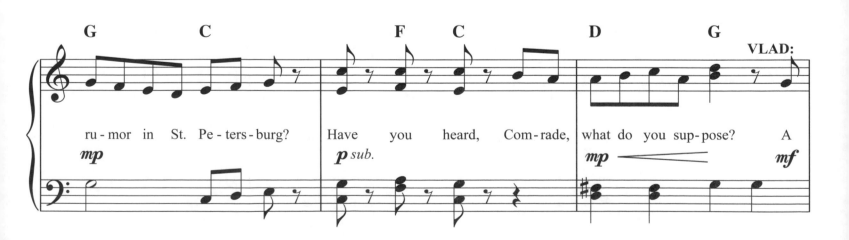

G   **C**   **F**   **C**   **D**   **G**

VLAD:

ru - mor in St. Pe - ters - burg?   Have you heard, Com - rade, what do you sup - pose?   A

mp   *p sub.*   *mp*   *mf*

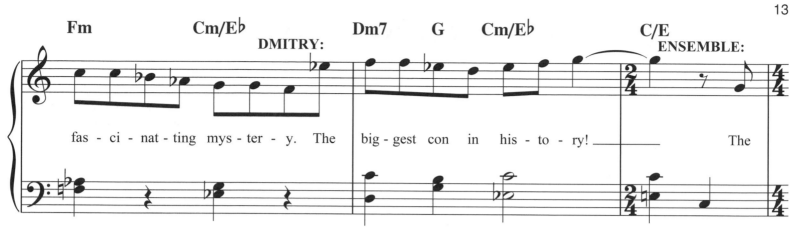

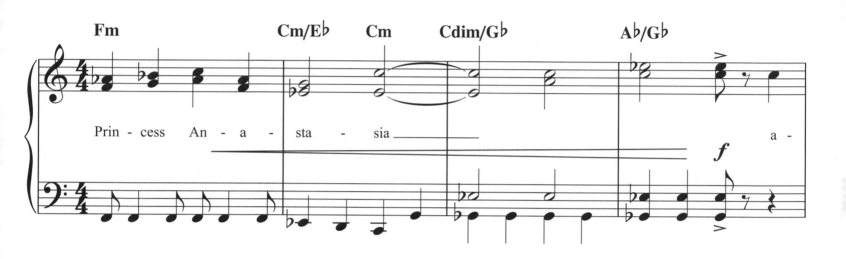

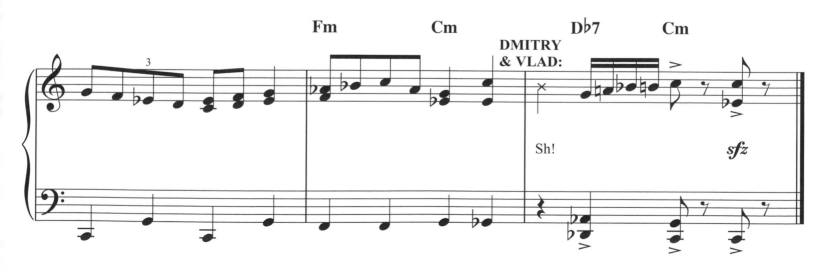

IN MY DREAMS

Lyrics by LYNN AHRENS
Music by STEPHEN FLAHERTY

darkness and cold _____ with the wind in the trees, _____ a

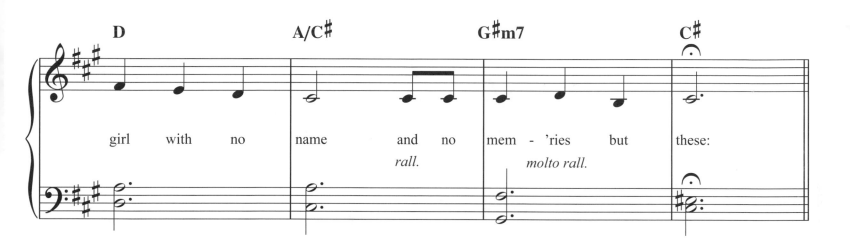

girl with no name and no mem - 'ries but these:

rall. *molto rall.*

With movement

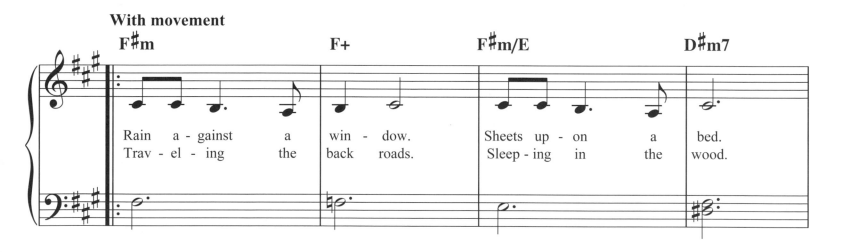

Rain a - gainst a win - dow. Sheets up - on a bed.
Trav - el - ing the back roads. Sleep - ing in the wood.

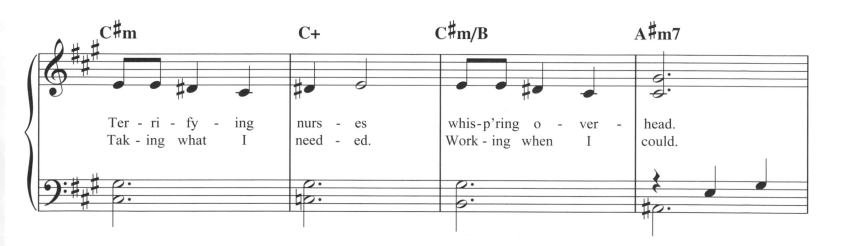

Ter - ri - fy - ing nurs - es whis - p'ring o - ver - head.
Tak - ing what I need - ed. Work - ing when I could.

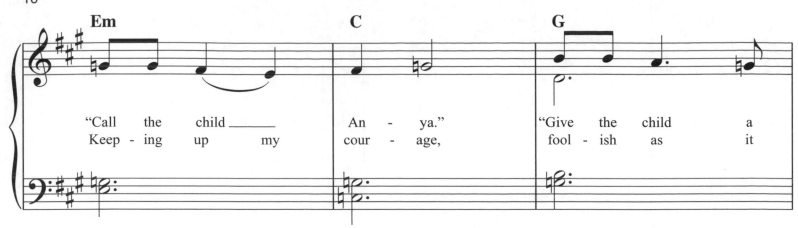

"Call the child _____ An - ya."
Keep - ing up my cour - age,

"Give the child a hat." I
fool - ish as it seems, at

hat." I don't know a thing be - fore
seems, at night all a - lone, in my

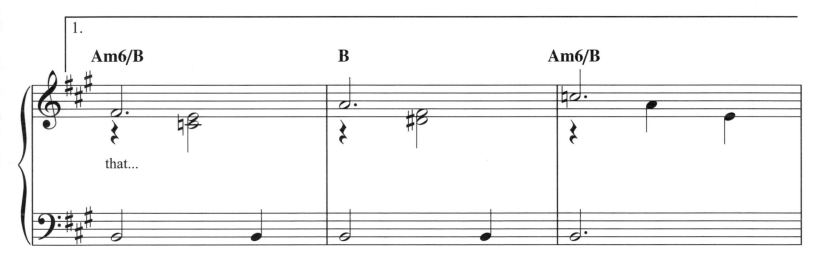

1.

that...

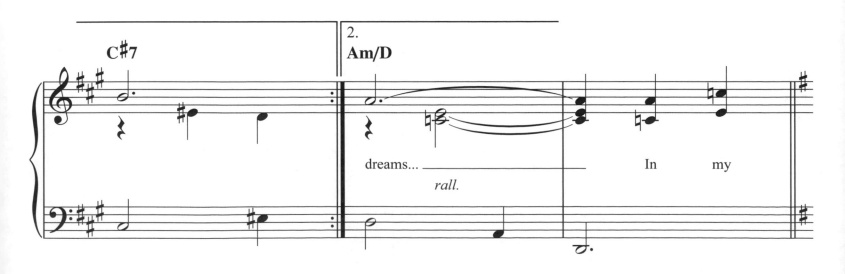

2.

dreams... _____ In my
rall.

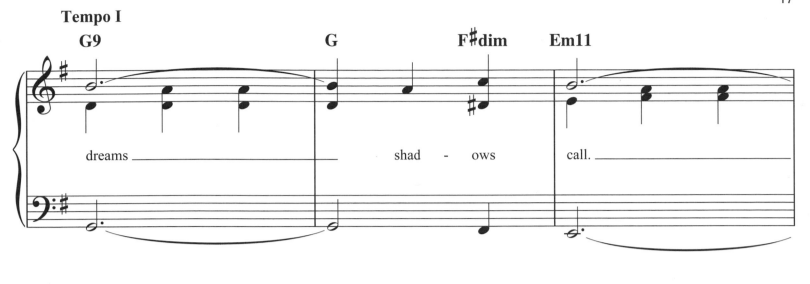

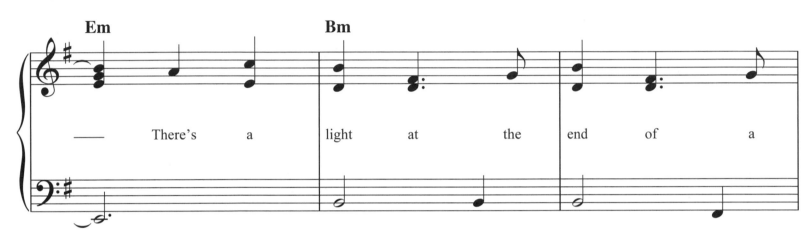

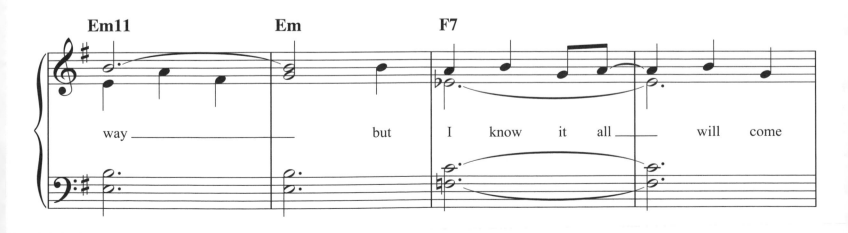

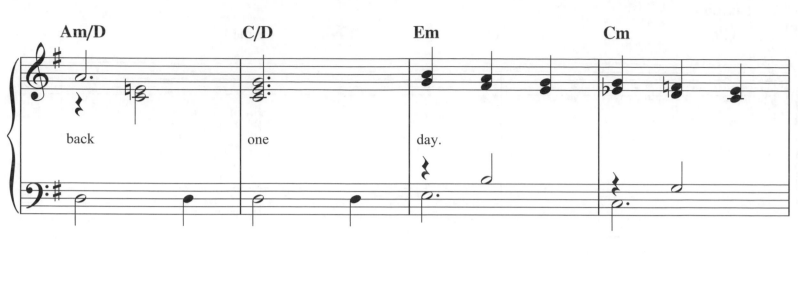

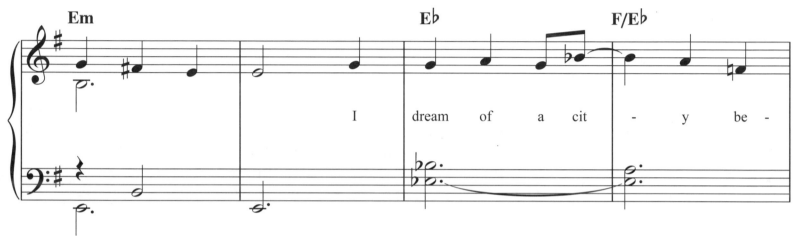

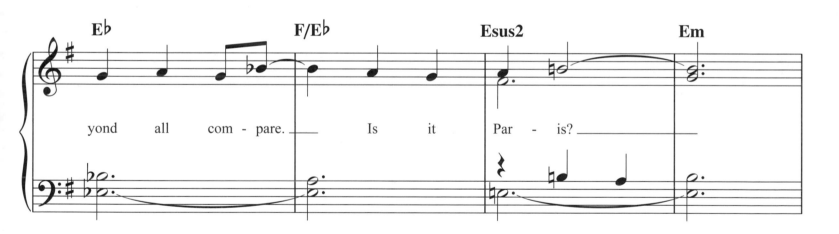

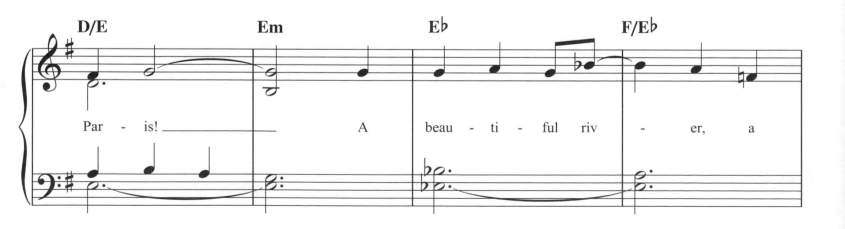

19

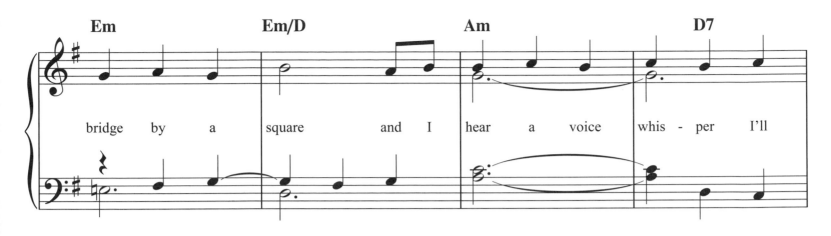

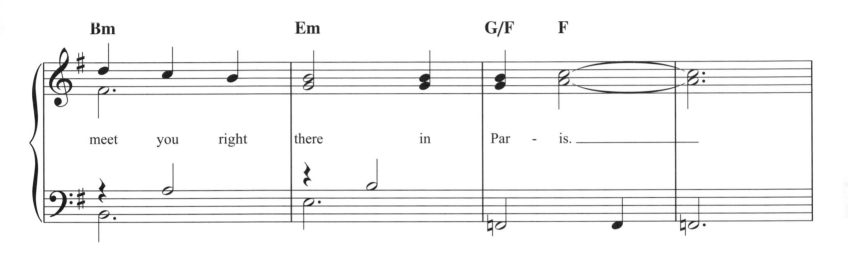

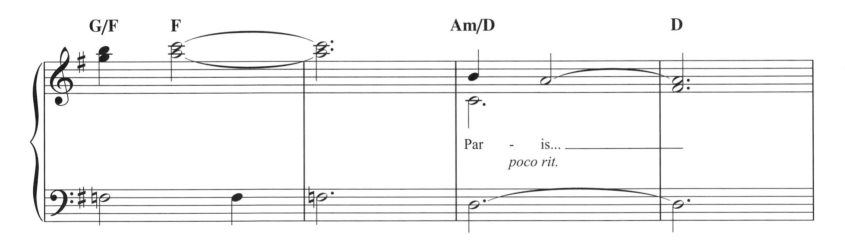

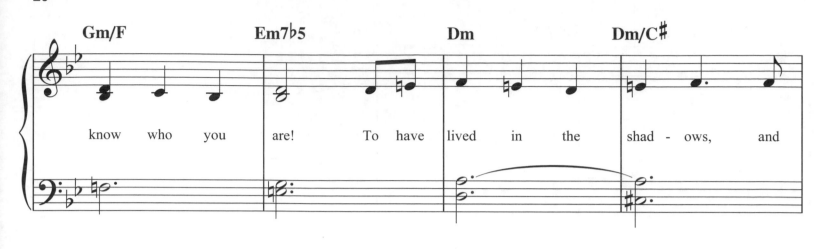

know who you are! To have lived in the shad - ows, and

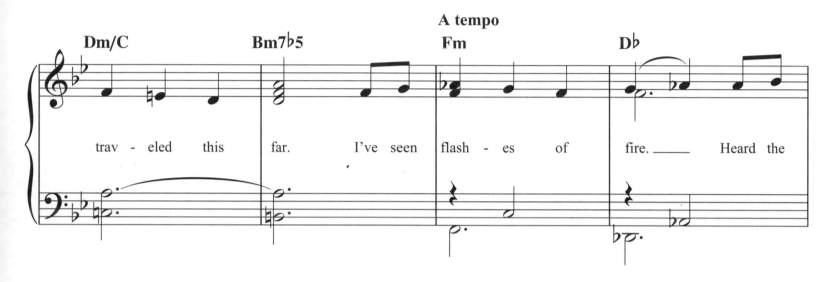

trav - eled this far. I've seen flash - es of fire._____ Heard the

ech - o of screams. But I still have this faith in the

truth of my dreams...

poco rall.

In my

molto rall.

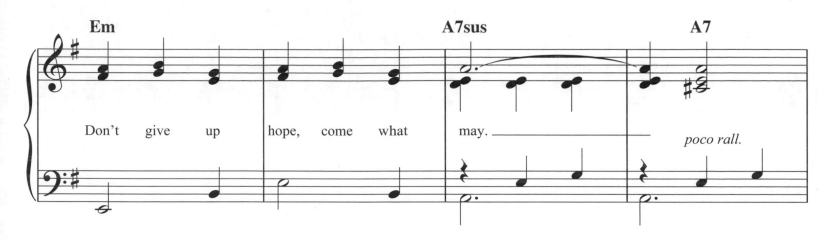

Don't give up hope, come what may. _____ *poco rall.*

Defiantly

I know it all will come back

With motion

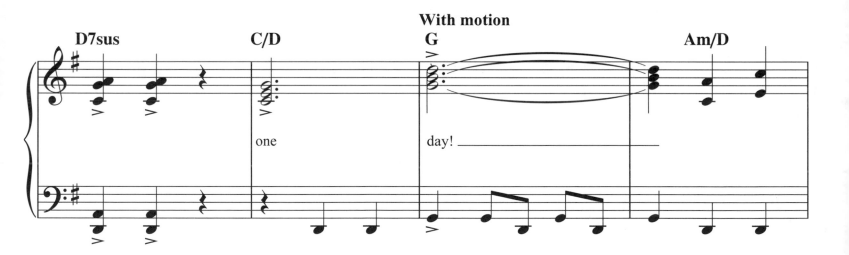

one day! _____

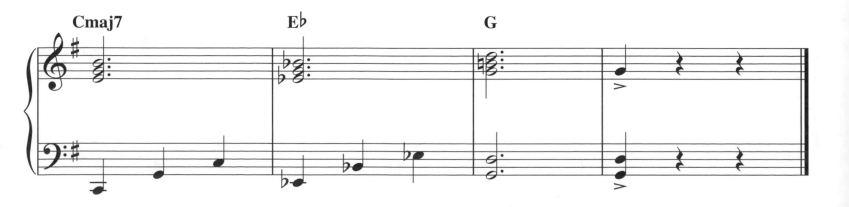

LEARN TO DO IT

Words and Music by LYNN AHRENS
and STEPHEN FLAHERTY

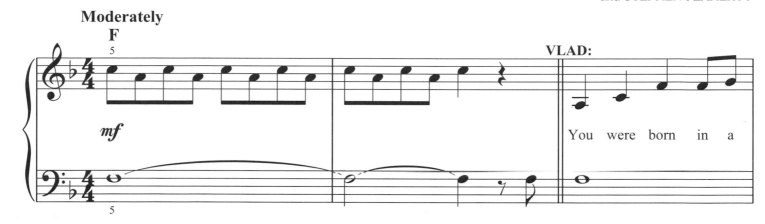

VLAD:
You were born in a

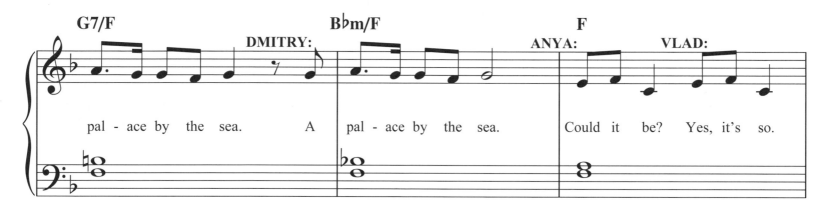

DMITRY: pal-ace by the sea. A pal-ace by the sea. ANYA: VLAD: Could it be? Yes, it's so.

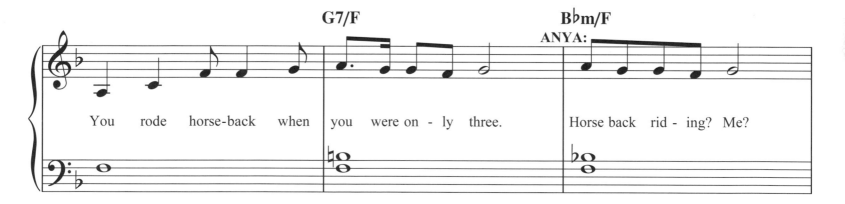

You rode horse-back when you were on-ly three. ANYA: Horse back rid-ing? Me?

DMITRY: VLAD: Hors-e's name? Ro-me-o! You threw tan-trums and ter-ror-ized the cook!

24

How the pal-ace shook! Charm-ing child! Wrote the book! But you'd be - have when your

fa - ther gave that look! I - mag-ine how it was. Your long for-got-ten past! We've

lots and lots to teach you and the time is go - ing fast!

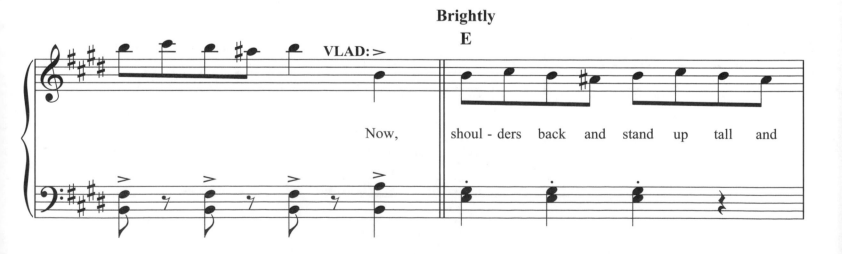

Now, shoul - ders back and stand up tall and

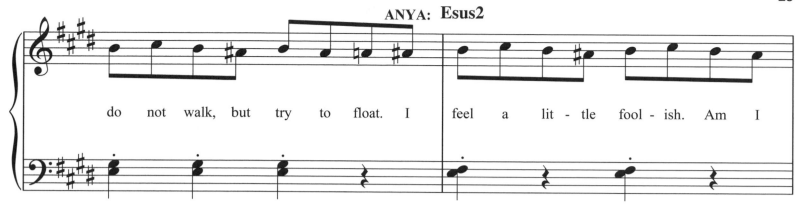

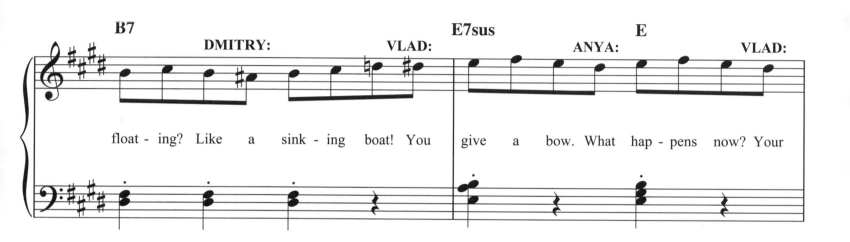

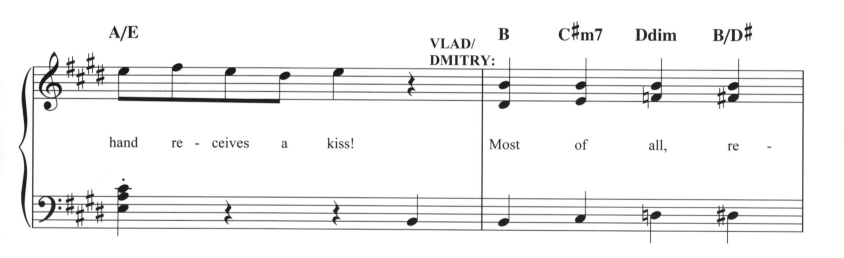

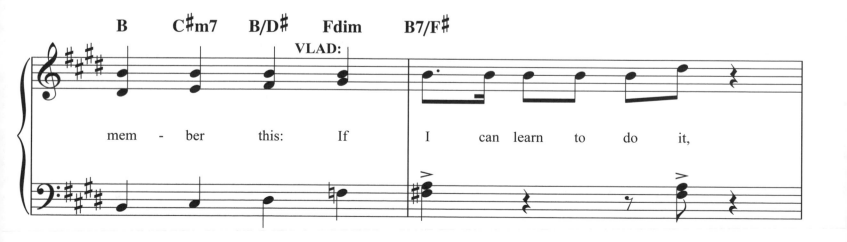

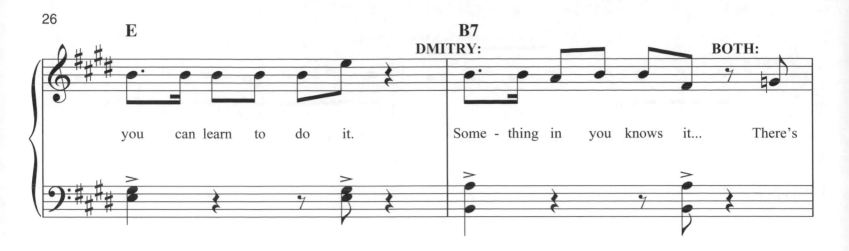

E   **B7**

DMITRY: BOTH:

you can learn to do it.   Some - thing in you knows it... There's

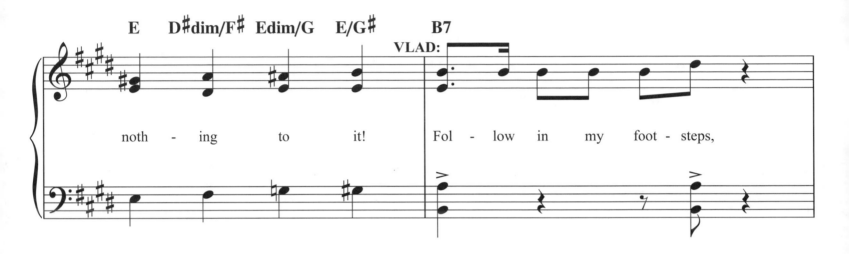

E   **D♯dim/F♯** **Edim/G** **E/G♯**   **B7**

                                       VLAD:

noth - ing to it!   Fol - low in my foot - steps,

E **D7** **C♯**   **F♯m**   **A**   **B7**   **E**   **C7**

                 BOTH: DMITRY:

shoe by shoe!   You can learn to do it, too!   Now,

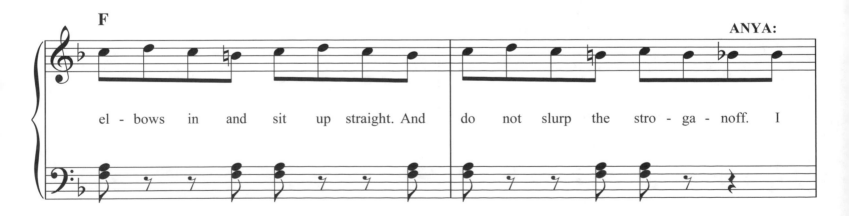

F   ANYA:

el - bows in and sit up straight. And   do not slurp the stro - ga - noff. I

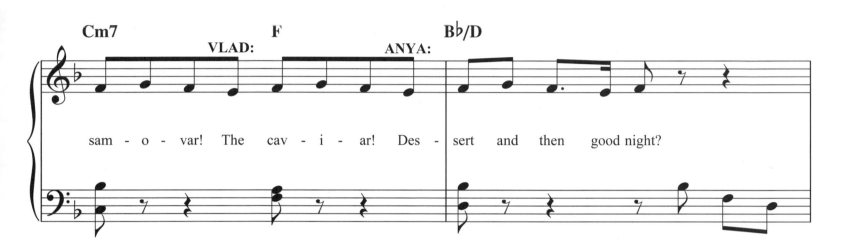

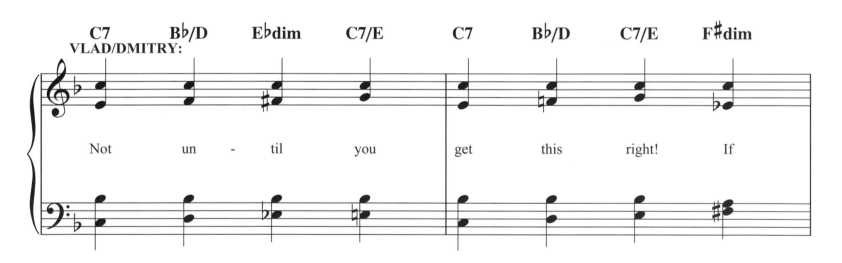

C7/E | **F** | **C7/G** | **G♯dim7** | **F/A**

Pull your-self to - geth - er and you'll pull through it!

C7/G | **F** | **E♭7** | **D7** | **Gm** | **B♭/C** | **C**

VLAD: Tell your-self it's ea - sy. **BOTH:** And it's true! You can learn to do it,

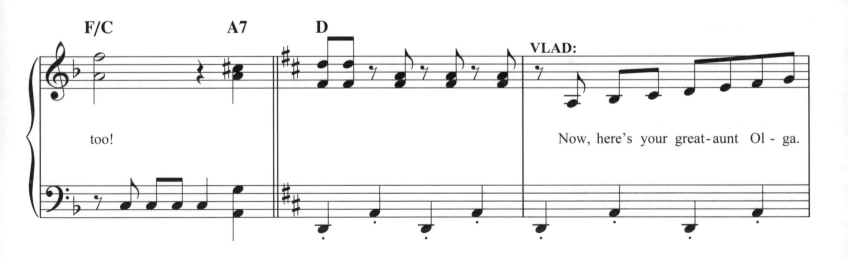

F/C | **A7** | **D**

too! **VLAD:** Now, here's your great-aunt Ol - ga.

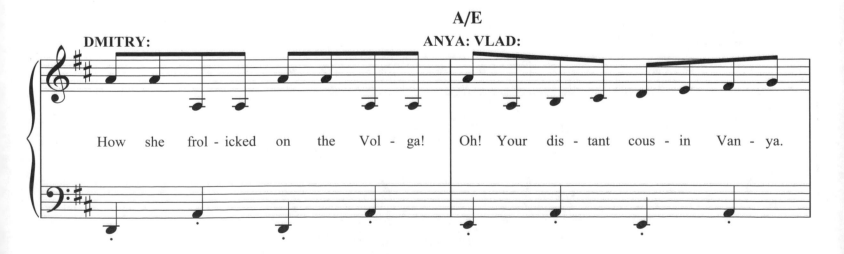

A/E

DMITRY: How she frol - icked on the Vol - ga! **ANYA: VLAD:** Oh! Your dis - tant cous - in Van - ya.

you can learn to do it,   he can learn to do it!   Pull your-self to-geth-er   and

we'll pull through it.   Tell your-self it's eas - y   and it's true!

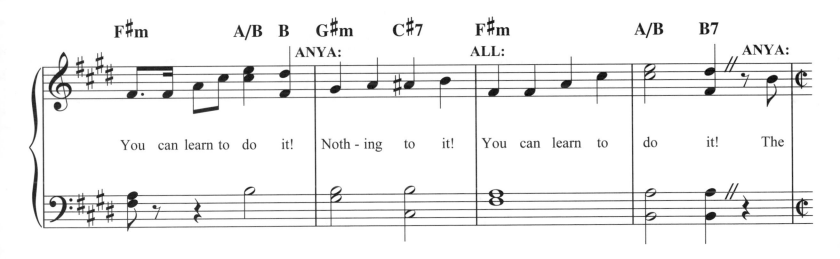

You can learn to do it!   Noth - ing to it!   You can learn to do it! The

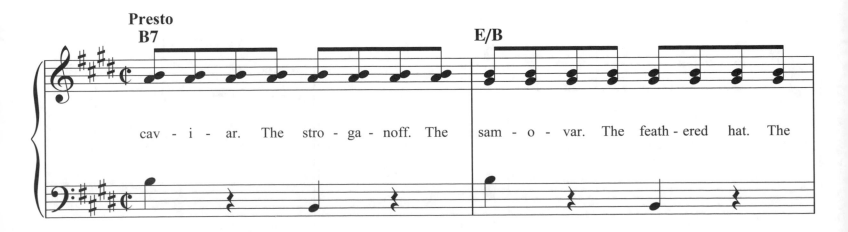

cav - i - ar. The stro - ga - noff. The   sam - o - var. The feath - ered hat. The

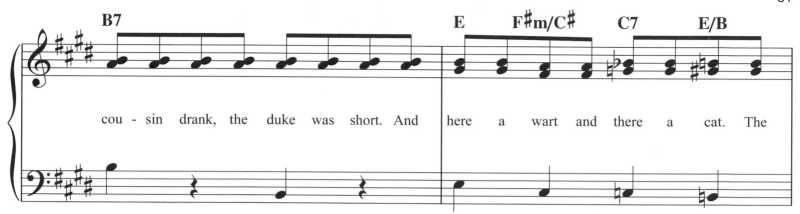

cou - sin drank, the duke was short. And here a wart and there a cat. The

hors - e's name was Ro - me - o. So tell me some-thing new! Ha! Ha!

You can learn to do it

too!

MY PETERSBURG

Lyrics by LYNN AHRENS
Music by STEPHEN FLAHERTY

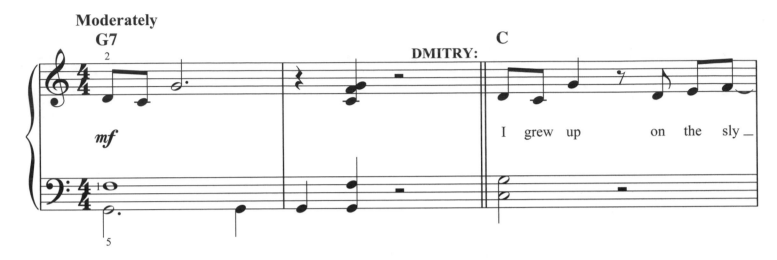

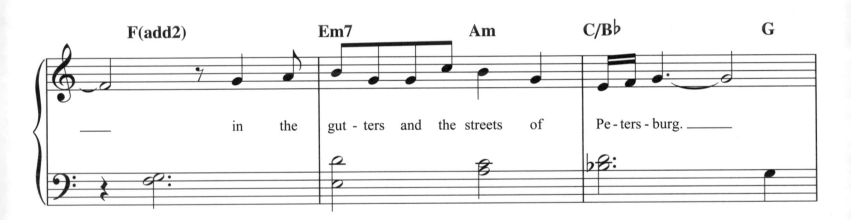

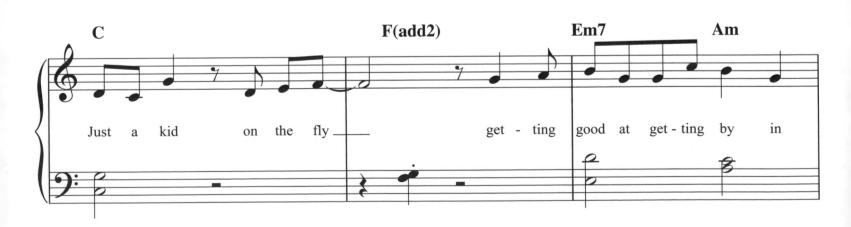

Pe-ters-burg. _____ I've bar-tered for a blan-ket, sto-

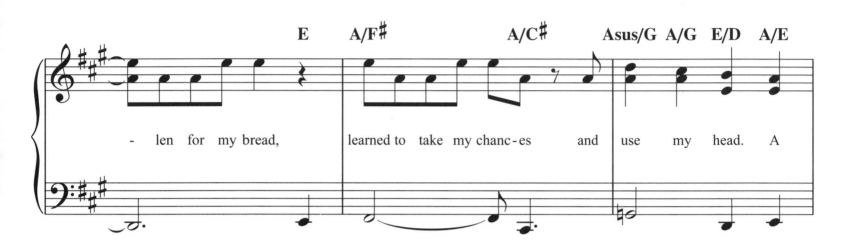

-len for my bread, learned to take my chanc-es and use my head. A

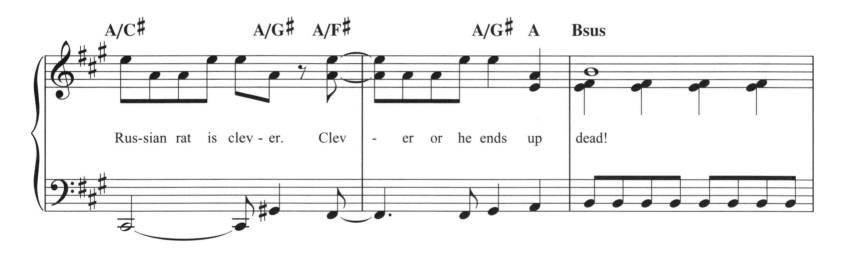

Rus-sian rat is clev-er. Clev - er or he ends up dead!

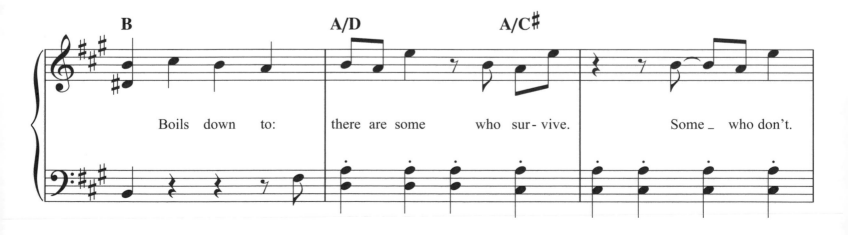

Boils down to: there are some who sur-vive. Some _ who don't.

Some give up. Some give in. ___ Me, ___ I won't! Black and blue, wel-come to ___

___ my Pe - ters - burg.

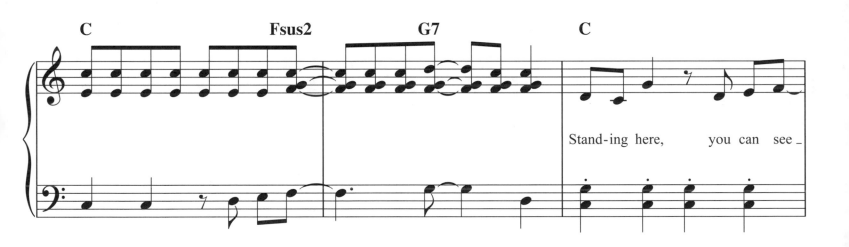

Stand-ing here, you can see ___

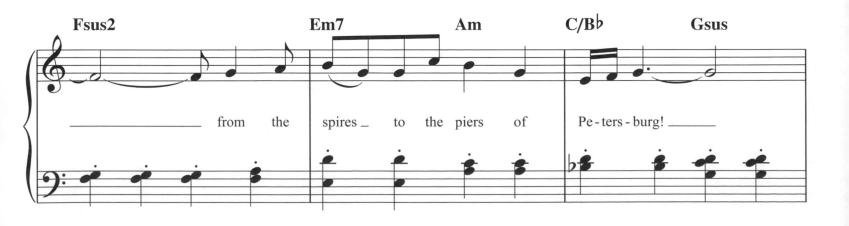

___ from the spires ___ to the piers of Pe - ters - burg! ___

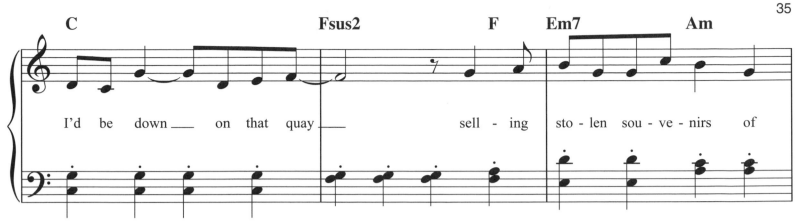

I'd be down ___ on that quay ___ sell - ing sto - len sou - ve - nirs of

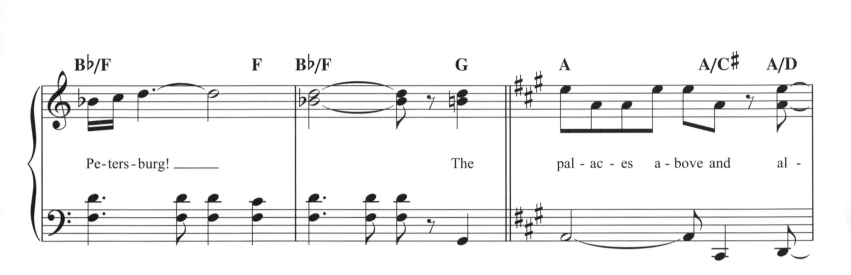

Pe - ters - burg! _____ The pal - ac - es a - bove and al -

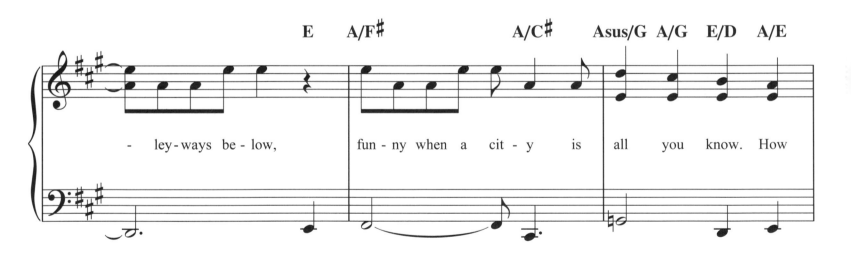

- ley - ways be - low, fun - ny when a cit - y is all you know. How

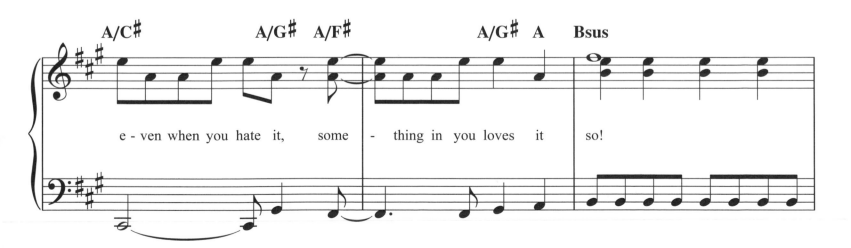

e - ven when you hate it, some - thing in you loves it so!

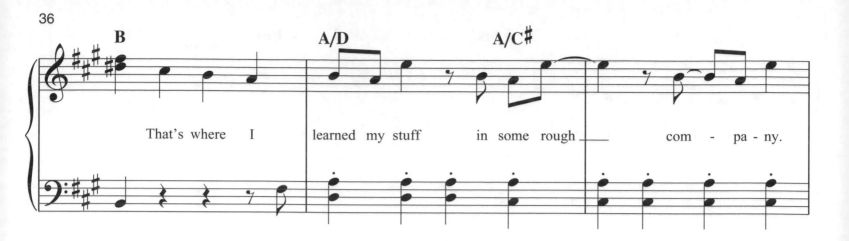

That's where I learned my stuff in some rough _____ com - pa - ny.

There's the boy _____ grow-ing up _____ who _ was me. All I've been, all I'll be. _

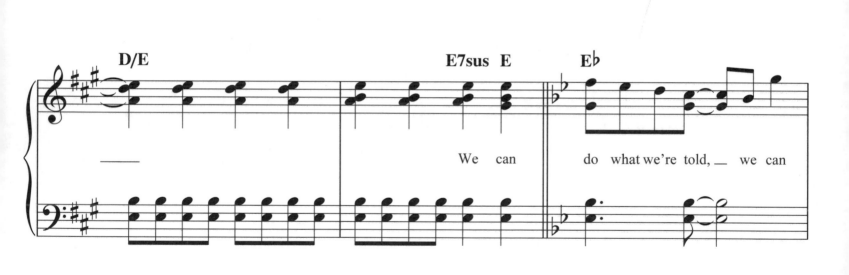

_____ We can do what we're told, _ we can

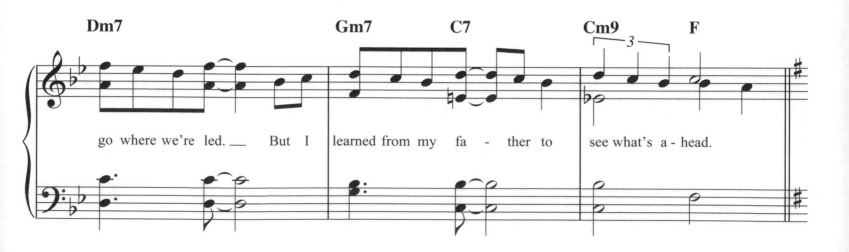

go where we're led. _ But I learned from my fa - ther to see what's a - head.

Noth-ing here to hold me. No ___ one that I owe. Fun-ny how a boy can

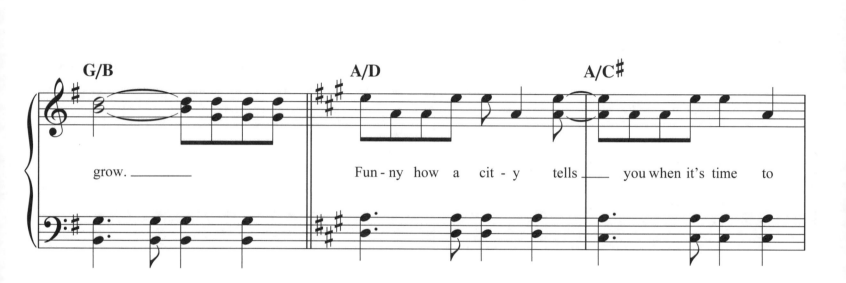

grow. ___ Fun-ny how a cit-y tells ___ you when it's time to

go! Boils down to: there are some who have walls ___

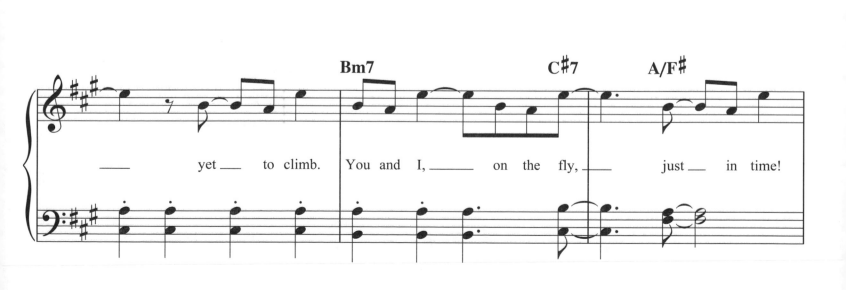

___ yet ___ to climb. You and I, ___ on the fly, ___ just ___ in time!

38

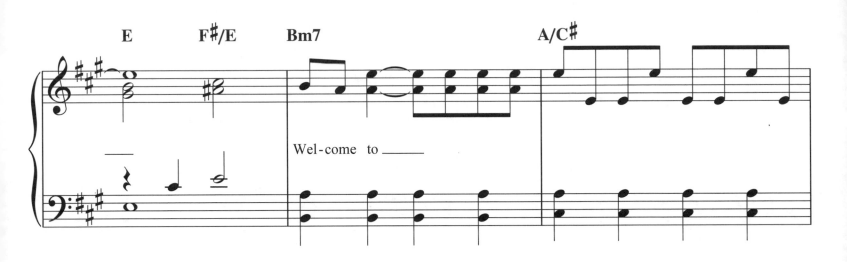

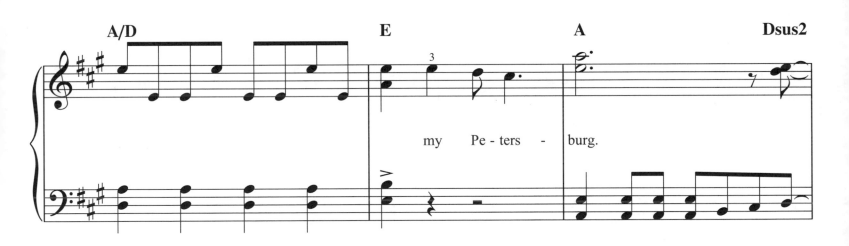

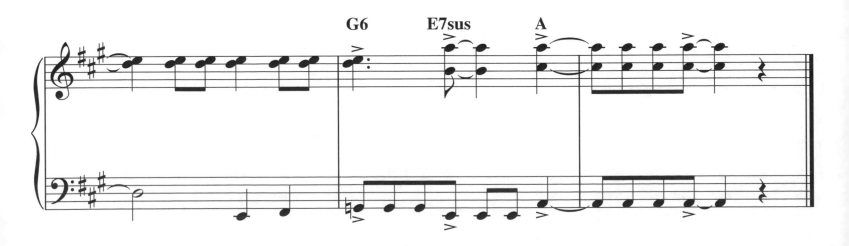

ONCE UPON A DECEMBER

Words and Music by LYNN AHRENS
and STEPHEN FLAHERTY

40

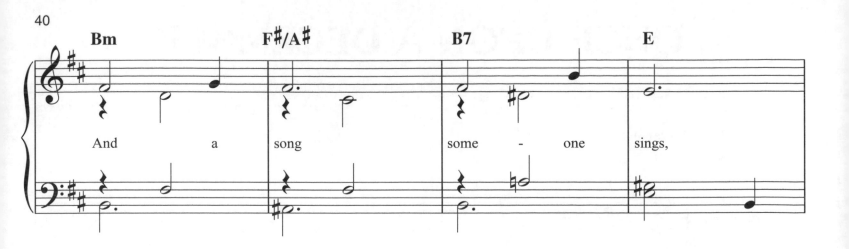

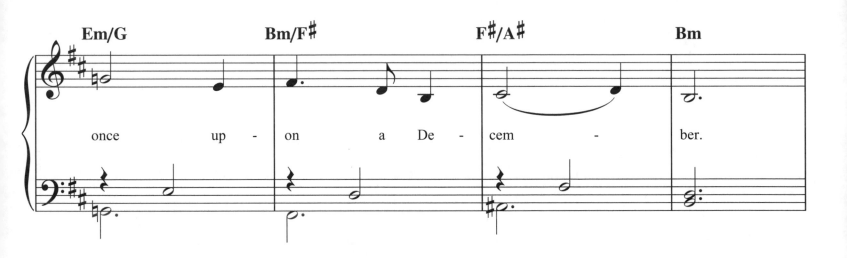

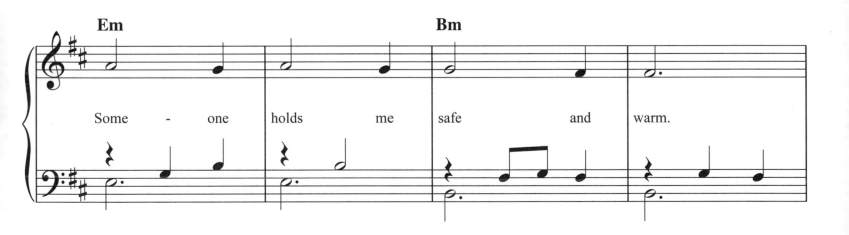

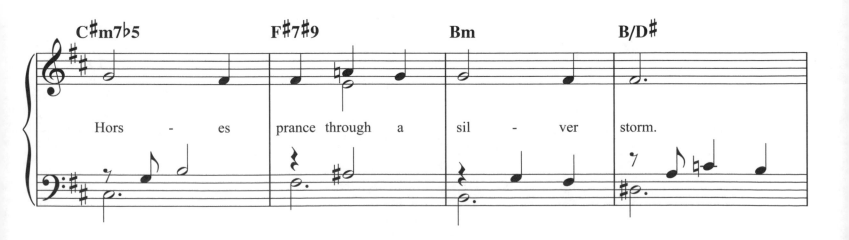

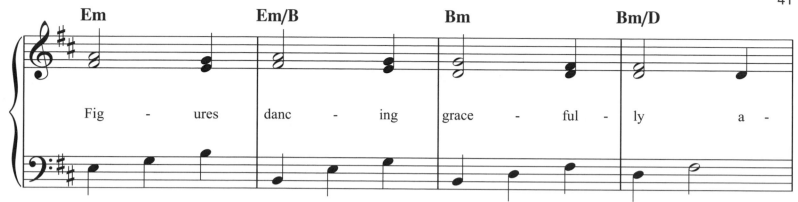

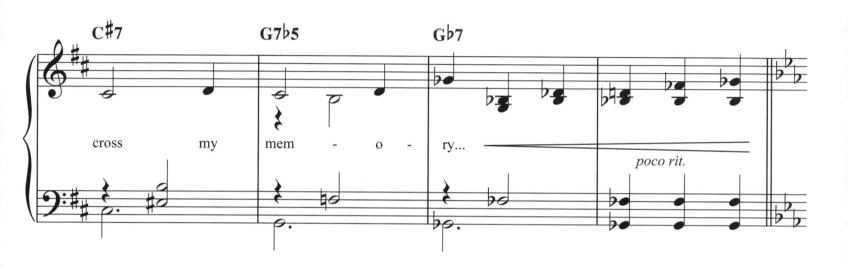

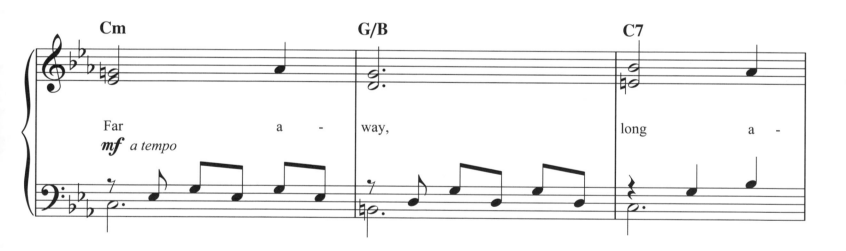

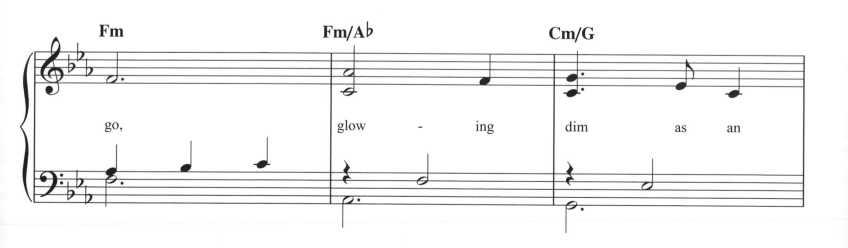

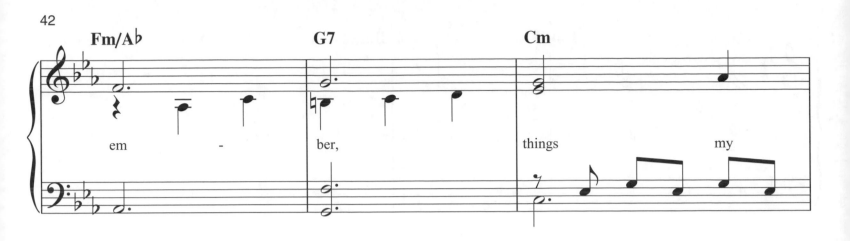

em - ber, things my

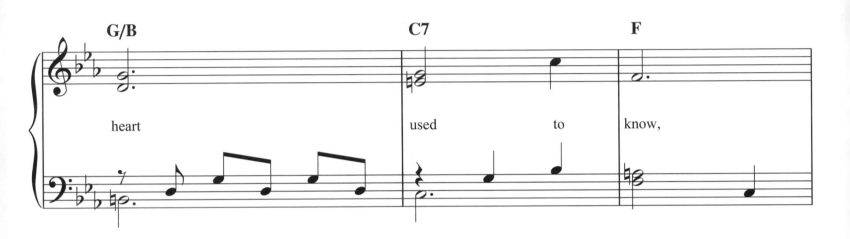

heart used to know,

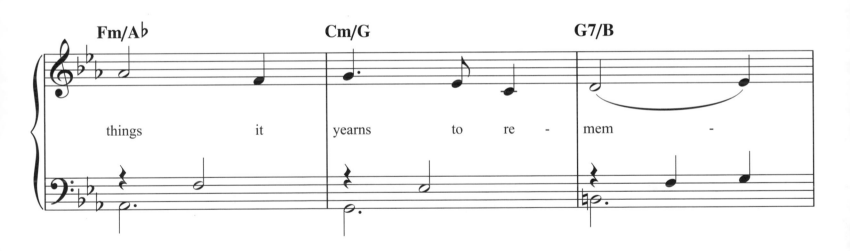

things it yearns to re - mem -

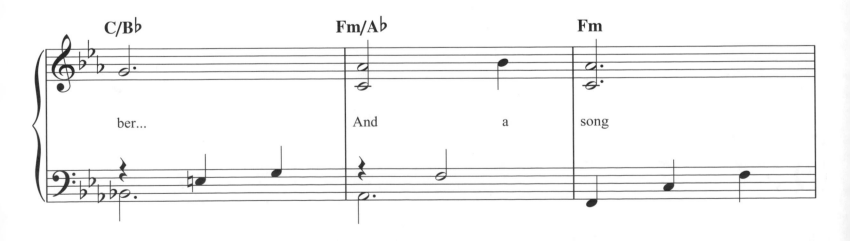

ber... And a song

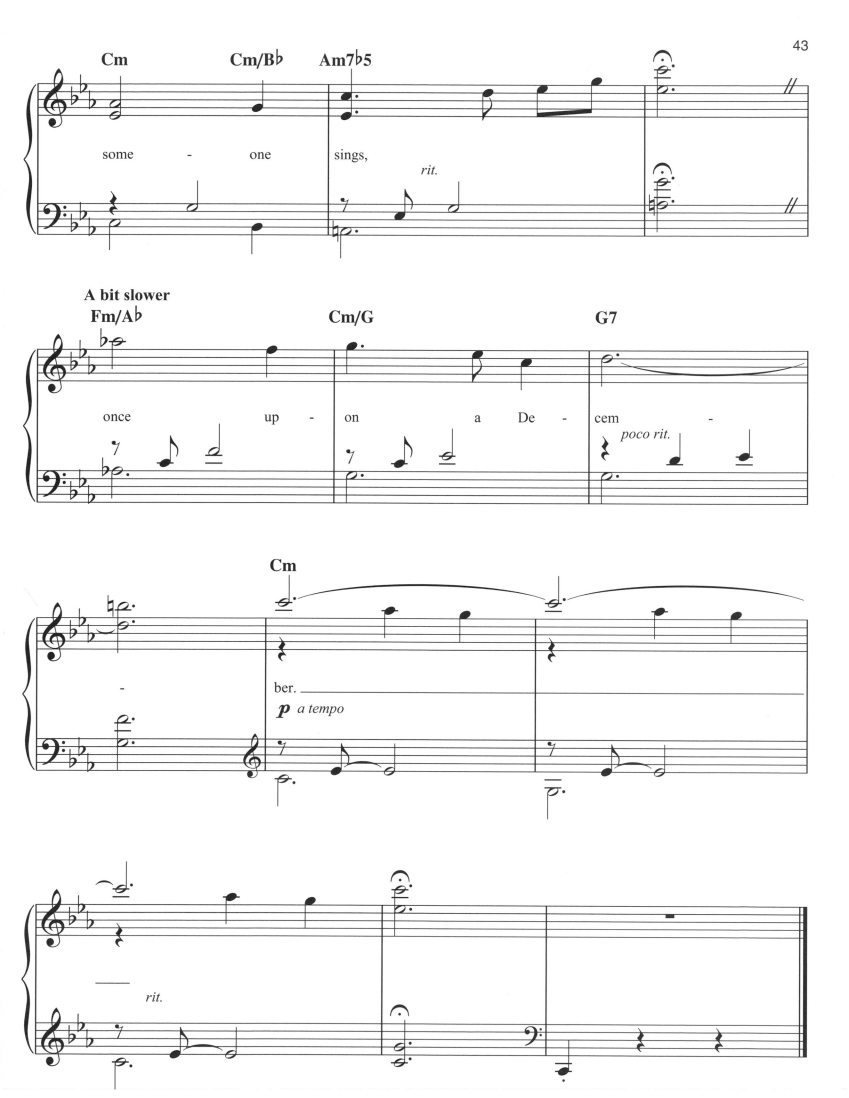

STAY, I PRAY YOU

Lyrics by LYNN AHRENS
Music by STEPHEN FLAHERTY

With feeling, freely

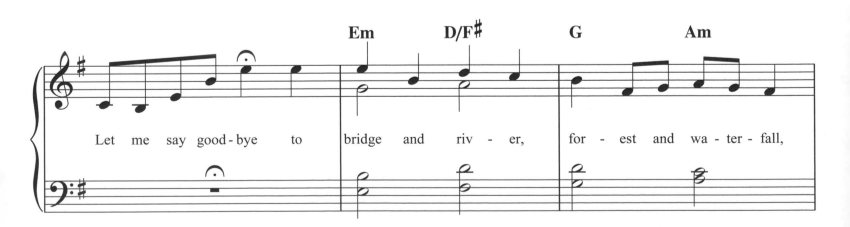

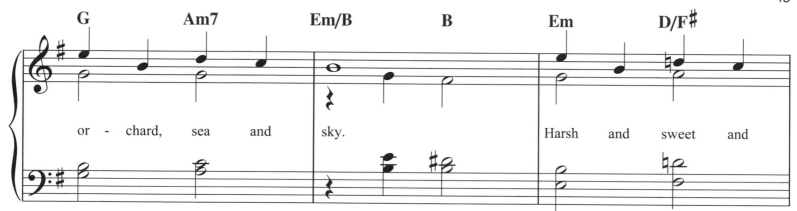

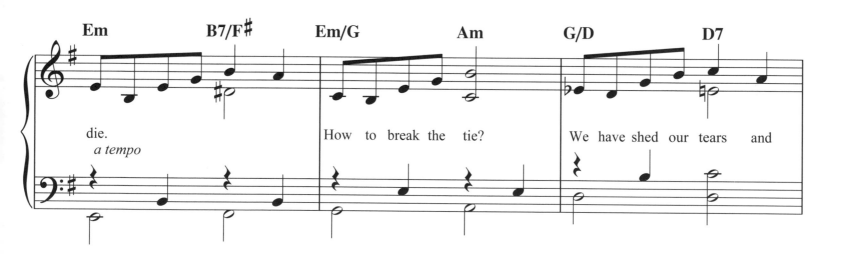

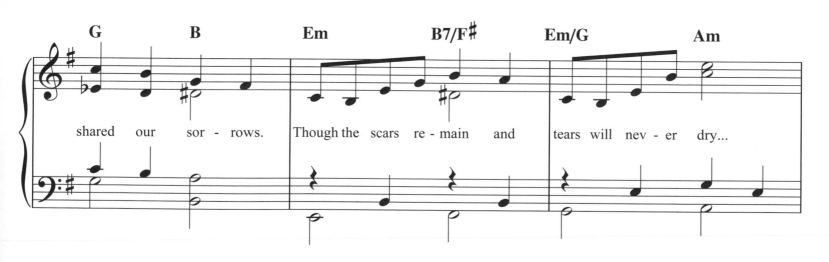

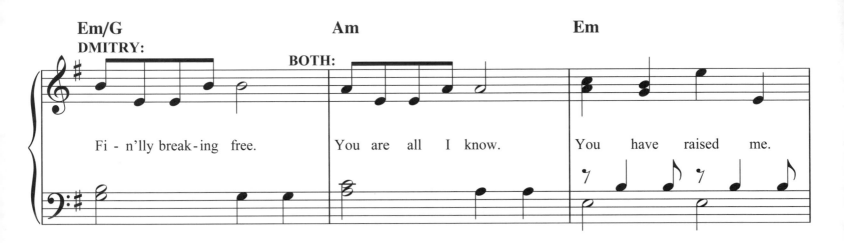

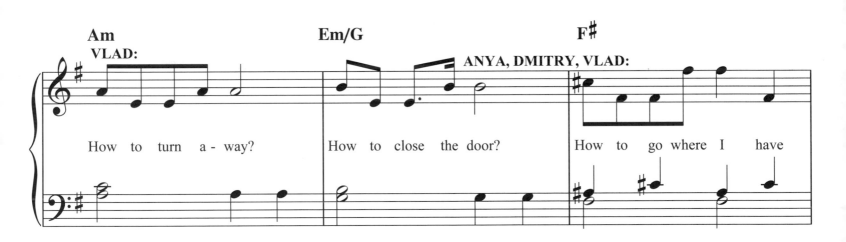

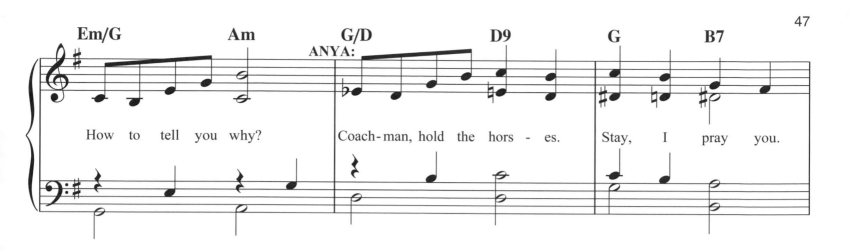

How to tell you why? Coach-man, hold the hors - es. Stay, I pray you.

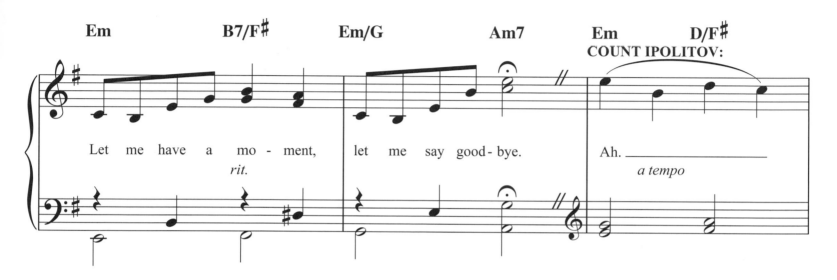

Let me have a mo - ment, let me say good - bye.

rit.

COUNT IPOLITOV:

Ah. _____

a tempo

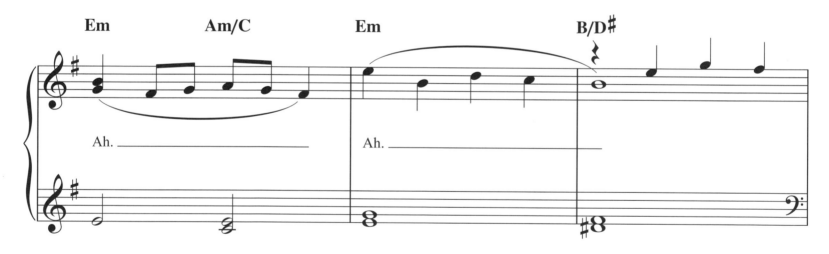

Ah. _____

Ah. _____

Harsh and sweet and bit - ter to leave it all. I'll bless my

ANYA, DMITRY, VLAD:

48

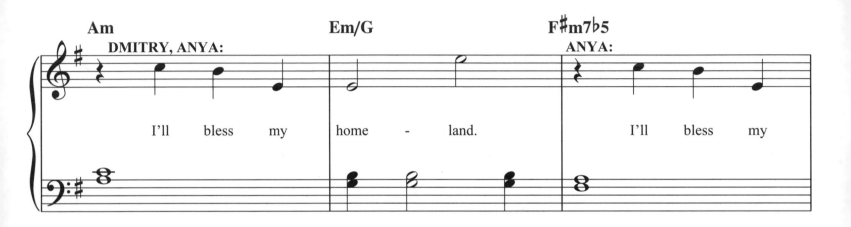

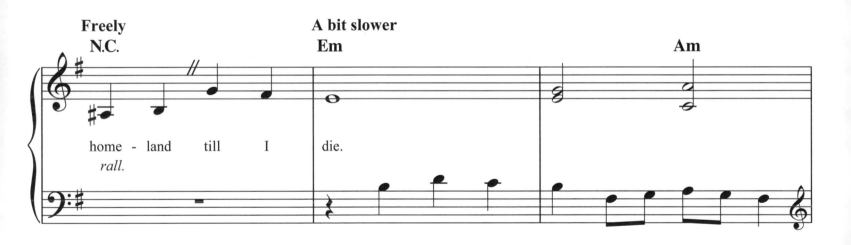

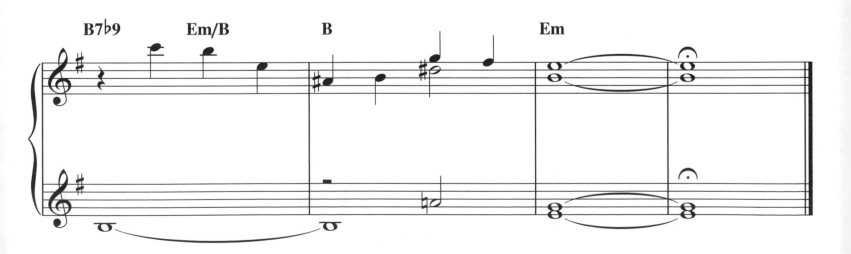

WE'LL GO FROM THERE

Lyrics by LYNN AHRENS
Music by STEPHEN FLAHERTY

We'll do some rem - i - nisc - ing, she'll see what

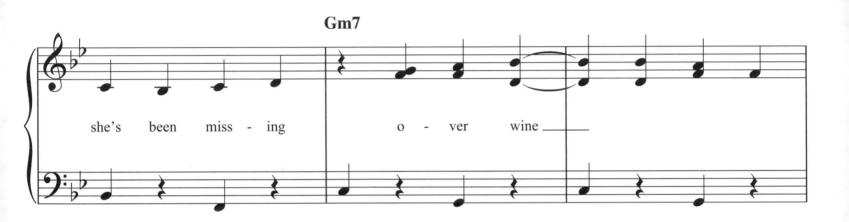

she's been miss - ing o - ver wine ___

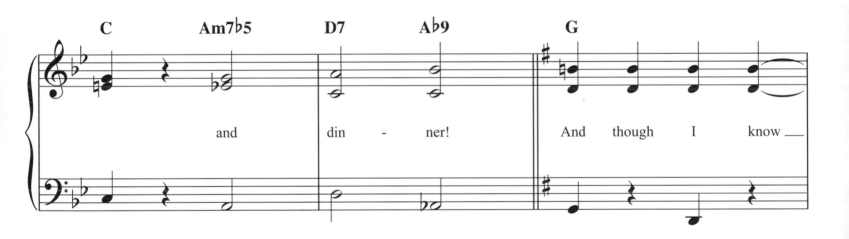

and din - ner! And though I know ___

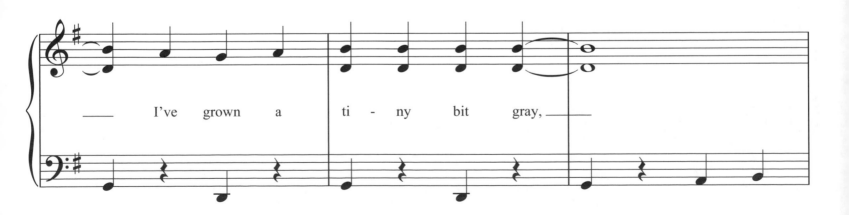

___ I've grown a ti - ny bit gray, ___

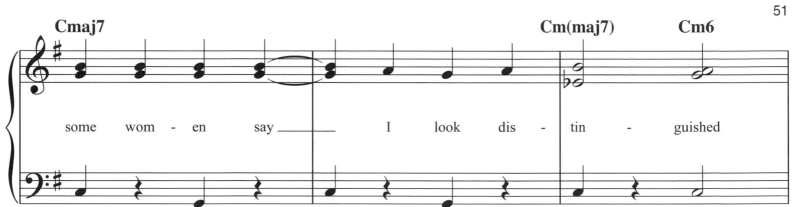

some wom - en say ____ I look dis - tin - guished

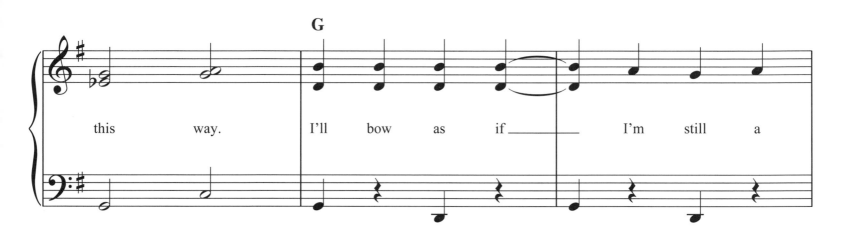

this way. I'll bow as if ____ I'm still a

frisk - y young pup. ____ Let's hope that I ____

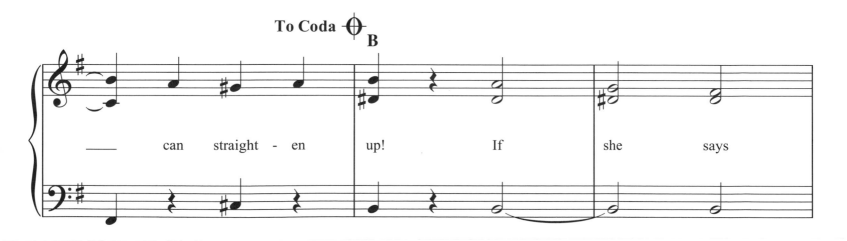

____ can straight - en up! If she says

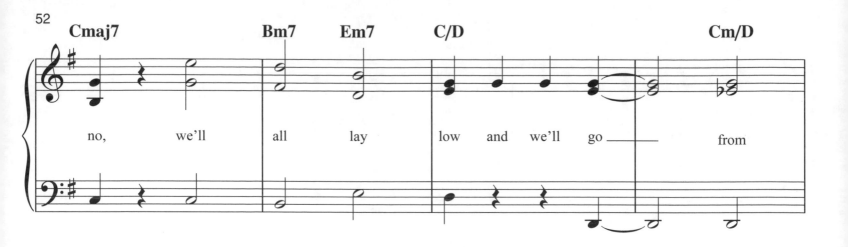

no, we'll all lay low and we'll go ——— from

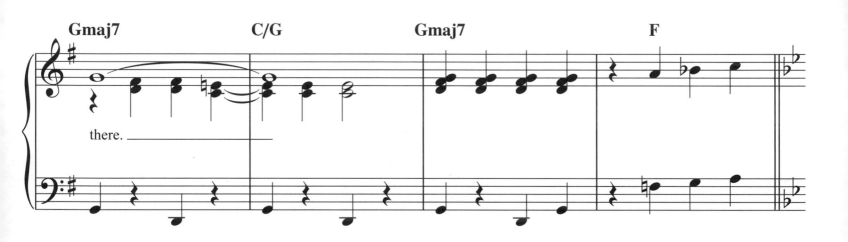

there. ———

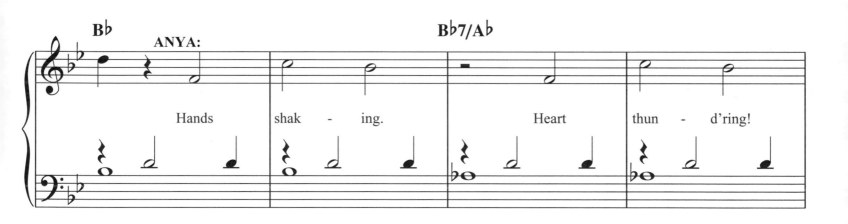

ANYA:

Hands shak - ing. Heart thun - d'ring!

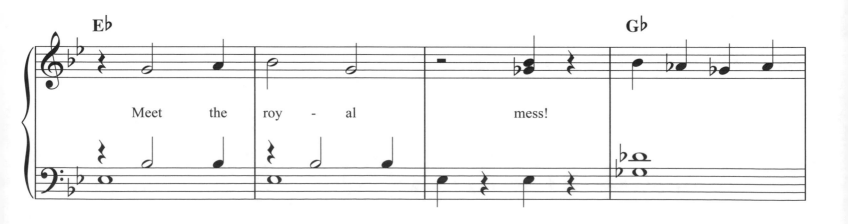

Meet the roy - al mess!

Start smil - ing. Stop won - d'ring

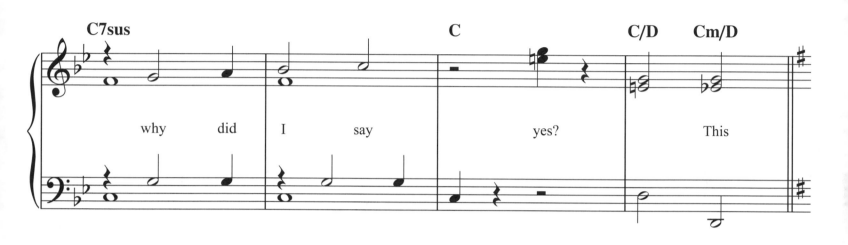

why did I say yes? This

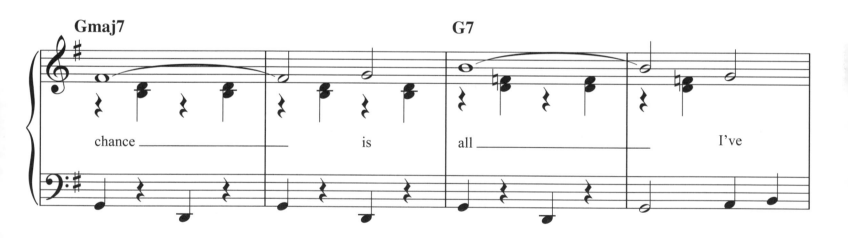

chance _____ is all _____ I've

got. _____ **DMITRY:** Keep a grip and take a deep breath and

54

soon ____ we'll know ____ what's

what. ____ Put on our

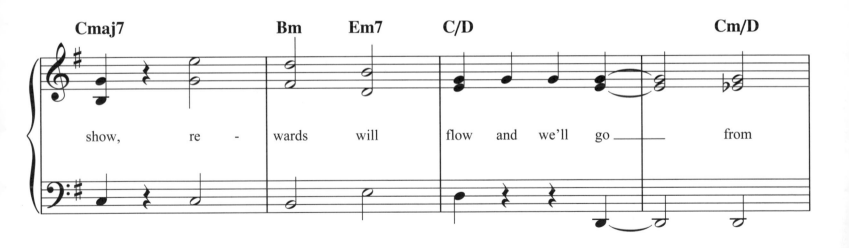

show, re - wards will flow and we'll go ____ from

ANYA: there. And we'll go ____ from

VLAD: there. And we'll go ____ from

55

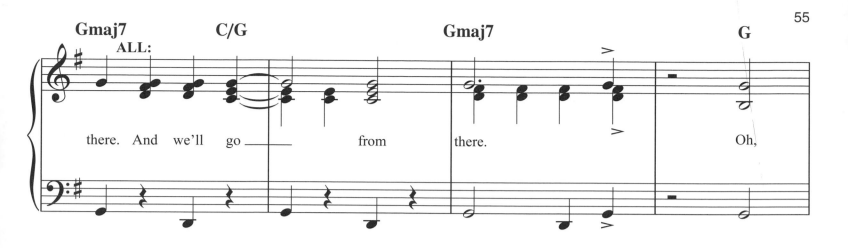

there. And we'll go _____ from there.   Oh,

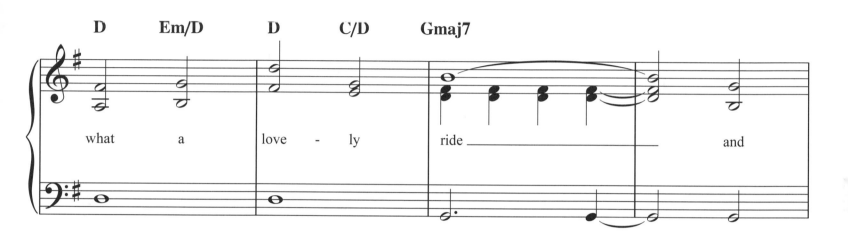

what a love - ly ride _____ and

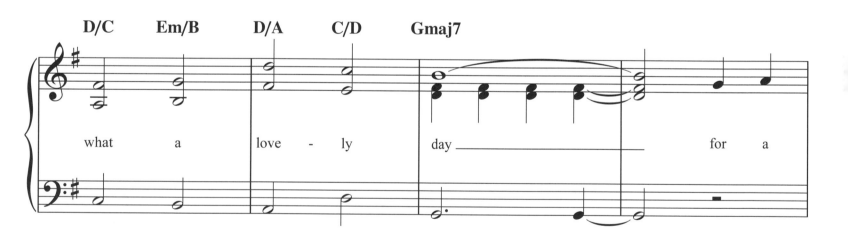

what a love - ly day _____ for a

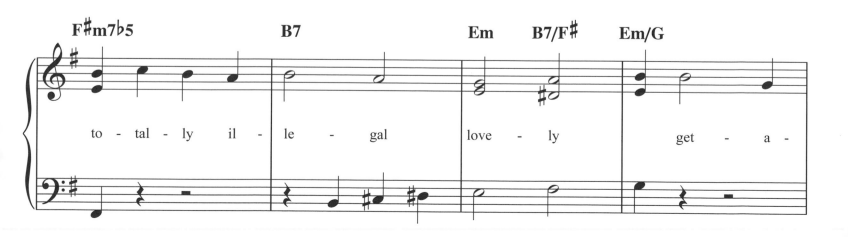

to - tal - ly il - le - gal love - ly get - a -

way!

Am7   Dsus   D   N.C.   **D.S. al Coda**

CODA

B   C   **DMITRY:**   Bm   Em7

up!   But   no   more   doubt!   No   time   to

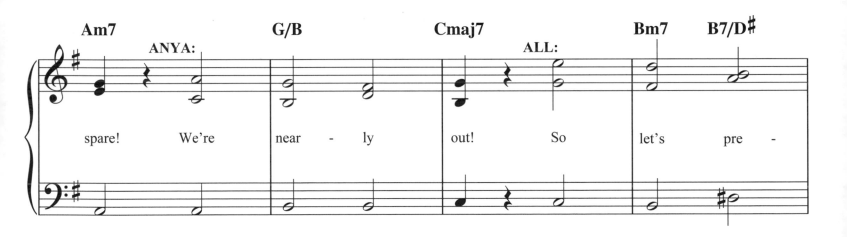

Am7   **ANYA:**   G/B   Cmaj7   **ALL:**   Bm7   B7/D#

spare!   We're   near - ly   out!   So   let's   pre -

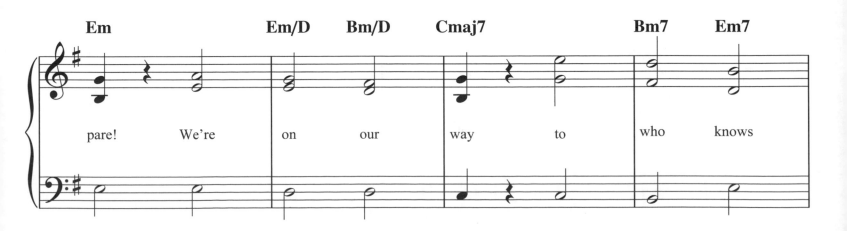

Em   Em/D   Bm/D   Cmaj7   Bm7   Em7

pare!   We're   on   our   way   to   who   knows

C/D   **A♭maj7**

where   and   we'll   go ____

and   we'll   go ____

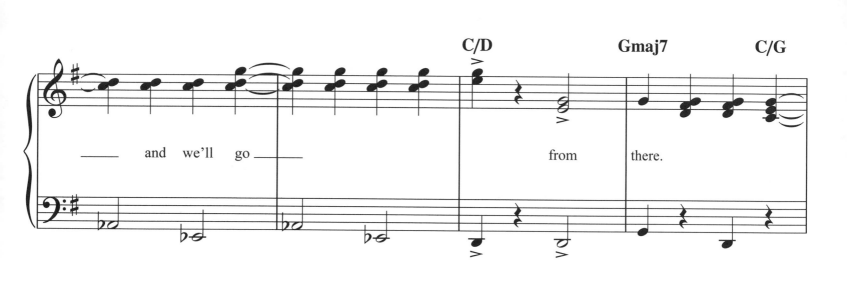

C/D   **Gmaj7**   **C/G**

____   and   we'll   go ____

from   there.

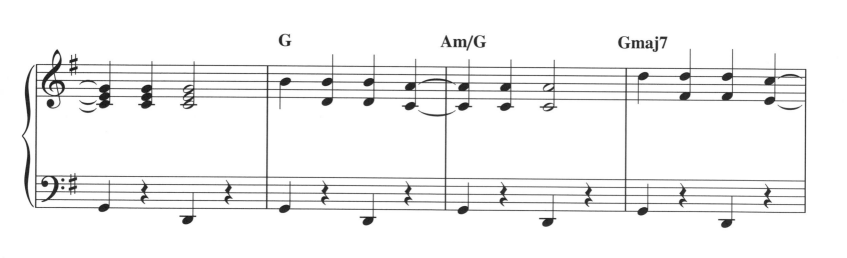

G   **Am/G**   **Gmaj7**

Am/G   **Am/D**   **G/D**   **G**

We'll   go   from   there.

STILL

Lyrics by LYNN AHRENS
Music by STEPHEN FLAHERTY

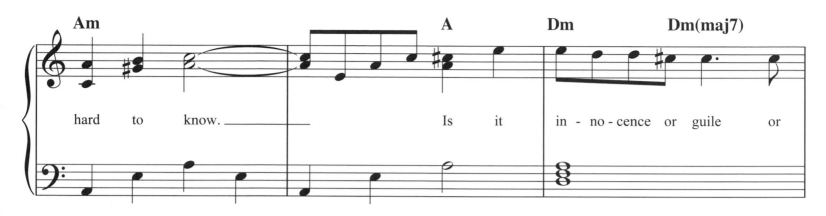

hard to know. _____ Is it in-no-cence or guile or

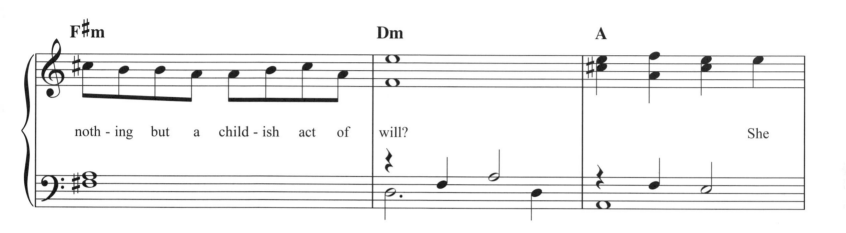

noth-ing but a child-ish act of will? She

does-n't know she needs you. She will-ful-ly mis-leads you but still...

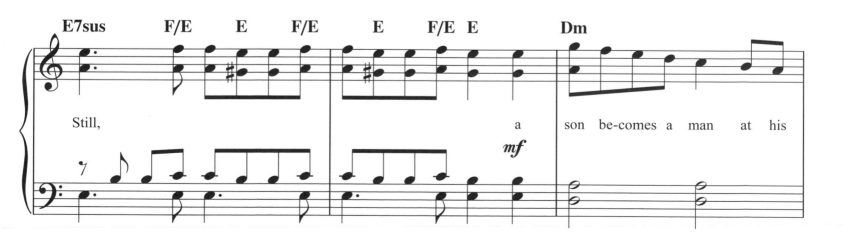

Still, a son be-comes a man at his

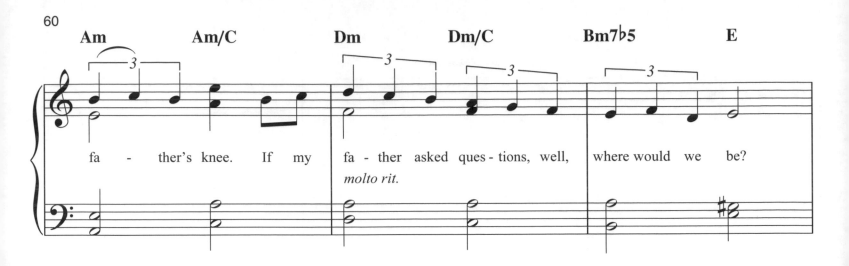

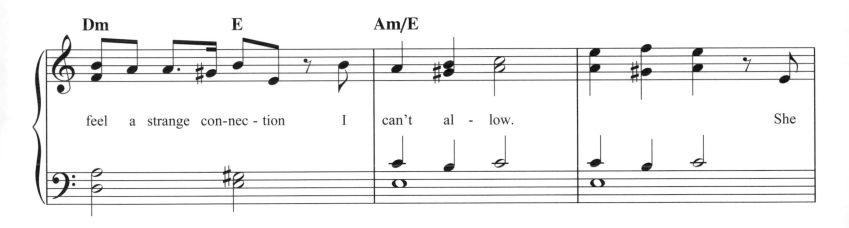

see that now. ____ I am noth - ing but a man with

noth - ing but his or - ders to ful - fill. "I'm

in - no - cent," she cries, but then you see her eyes, and some-thing in them tells you that she

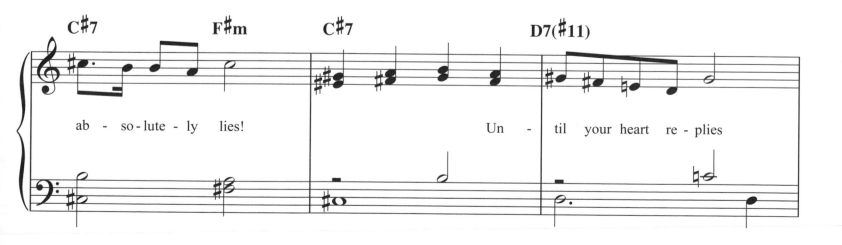

ab - so - lute - ly lies! Un - til your heart re - plies

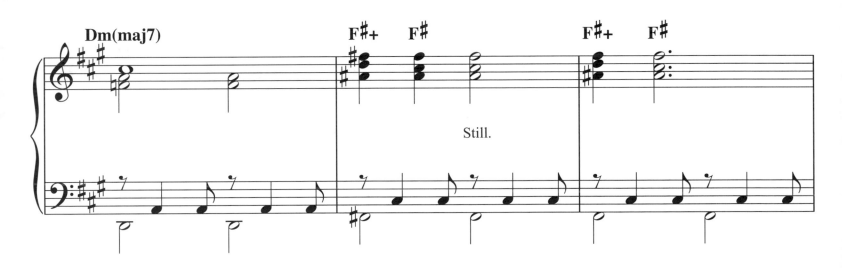

JOURNEY TO THE PAST

Words and Music by LYNN AHRENS
and STEPHEN FLAHERTY

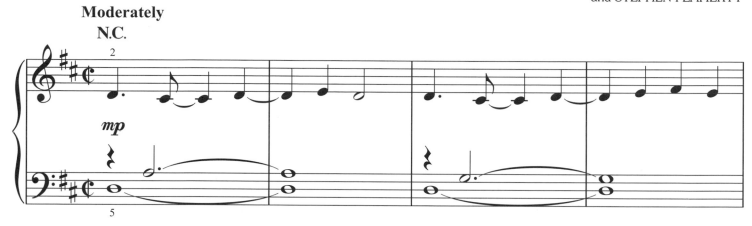

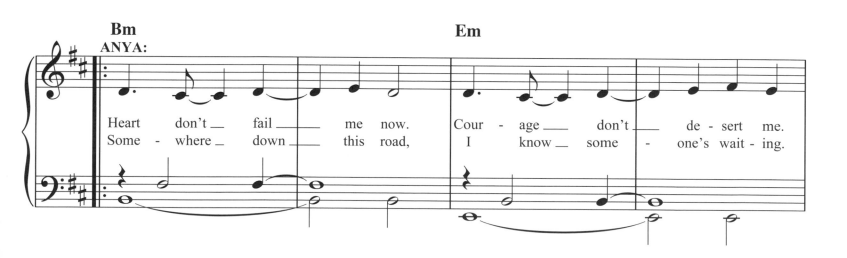

ANYA:

Heart don't __ fail __ me now. Cour - age __ don't __ de - sert me.
Some - where __ down __ this road, I know __ some - one's wait - ing.

Don't turn __ back __ now that you're here. __
Years of __ dreams __ just can't be wrong. __

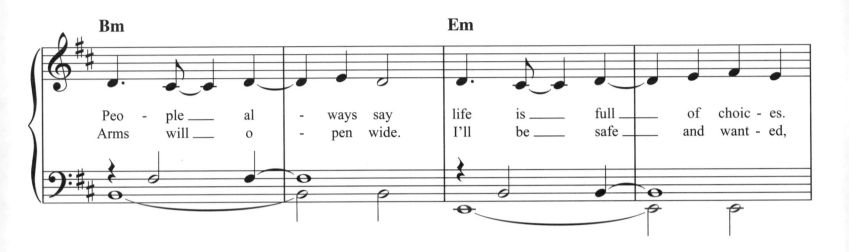

Peo - ple __ al - ways say life is __ full __ of choic - es.
Arms will __ o - pen wide. I'll be __ safe __ and want - ed,

No one __ ev - er men - tions fear __ or
fi - n'lly __ home __ where I be - long. __ Well,

how the __ road __ can seem so long.
start - ing __ here, __ my life be - gins.

How the ___ world ___ can seem so vast. _____
Start - ing ___ now, ___ I'm learn - ing fast. _____

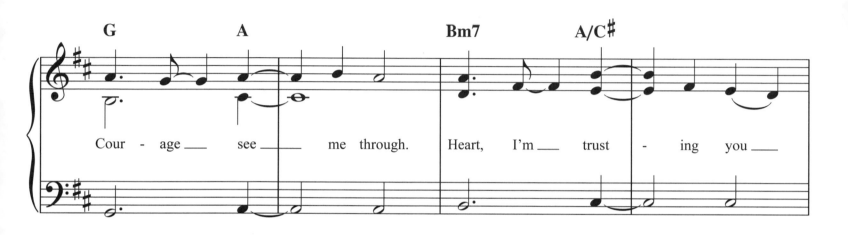

Cour - age ___ see ___ me through. Heart, I'm ___ trust - ing you ___

on this ___ jour - ney _____ to the

past.

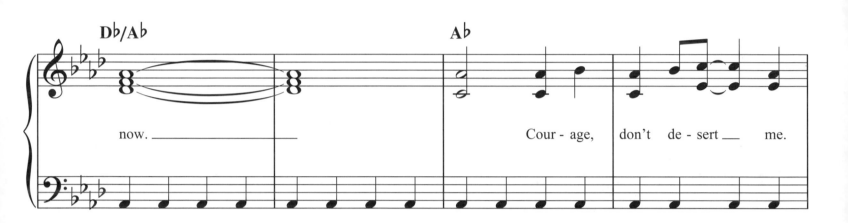

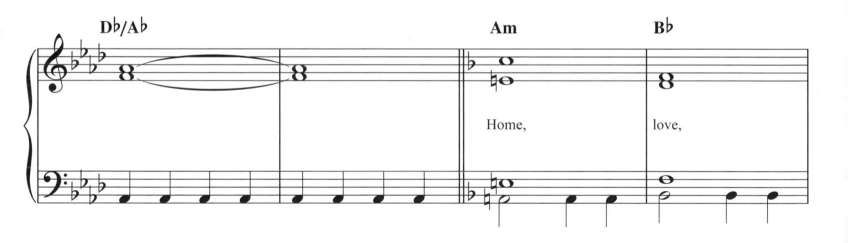

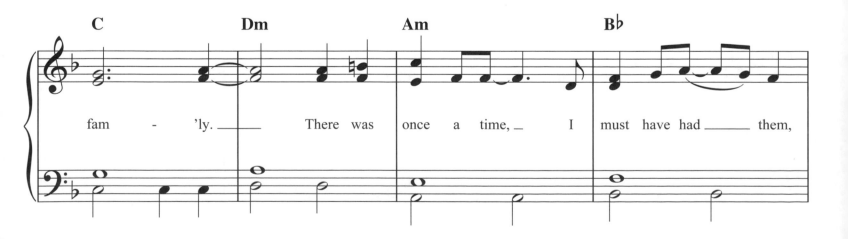

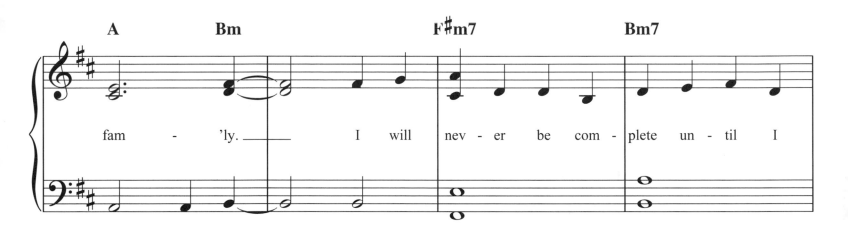

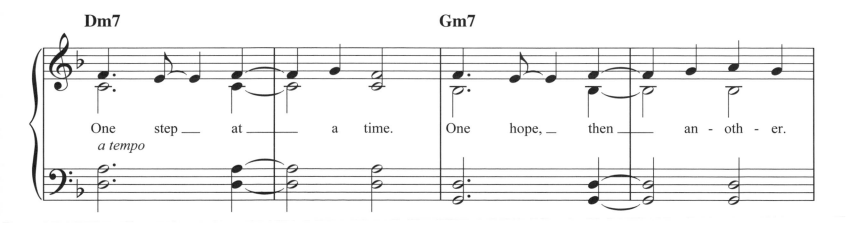

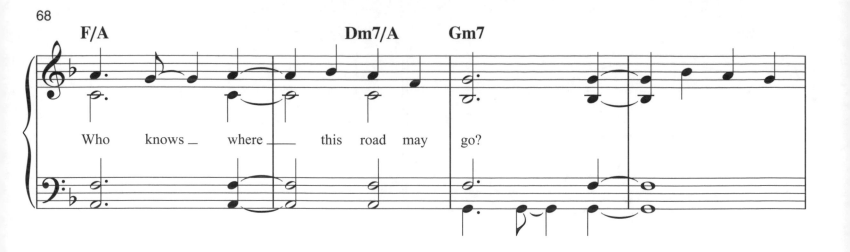

Who knows — where — this road may go?

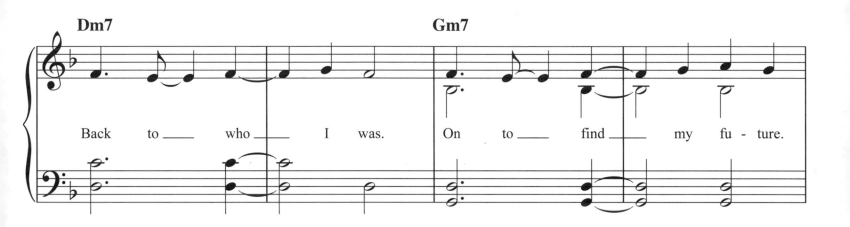

Back to — who — I was. On to — find — my fu - ture.

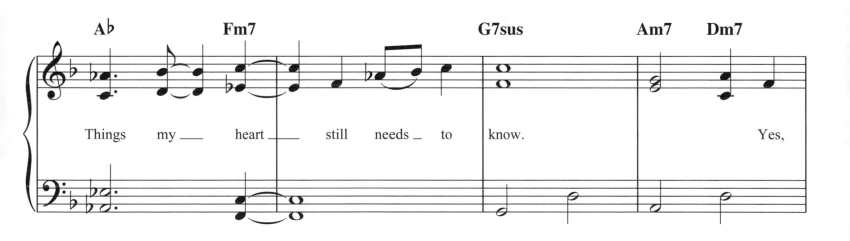

Things my — heart — still needs — to know. Yes,

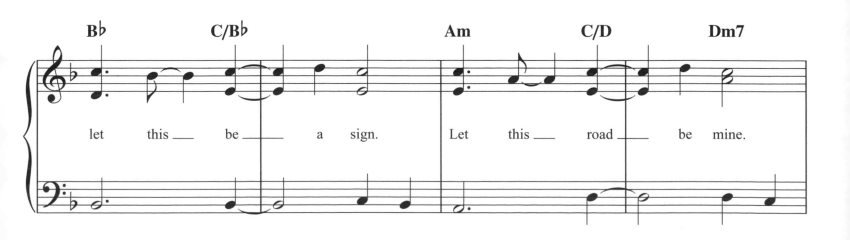

let this — be — a sign. Let this — road — be mine.

Let this —— lead —— me to my past, ————— and

bring me —— home ——

at —————

last.

rit.

PARIS HOLDS THE KEY
(To Your Heart)

Words and Music by LYNN AHRENS
and STEPHEN FLAHERTY

71

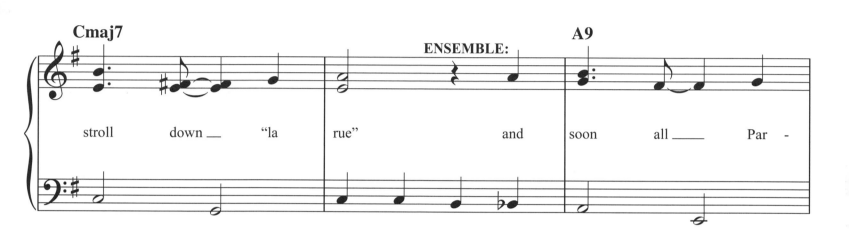

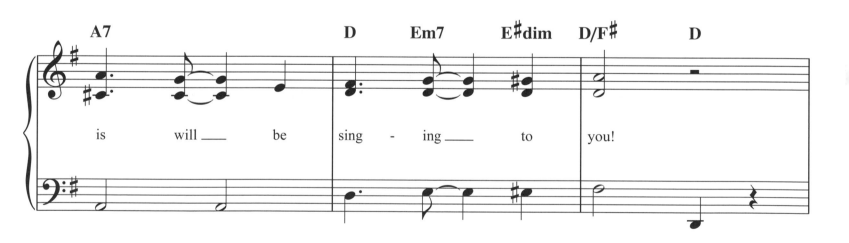

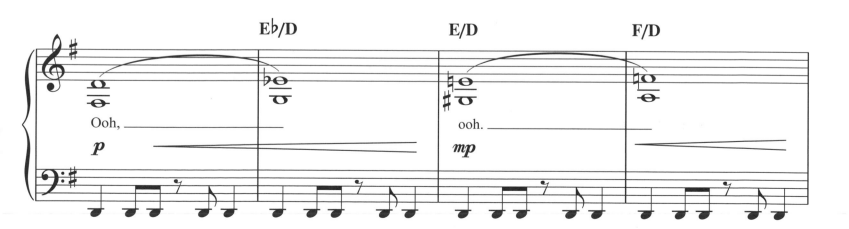

Ah. _____ Ah! _____ Par -

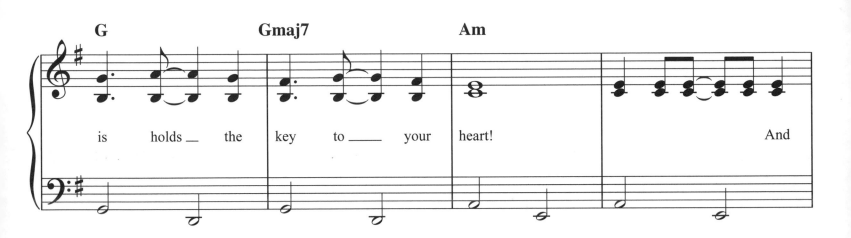

is holds ___ the key to ___ your heart! And

all of ___ Par - is plays ___ a part! Par -

is turned ___ a page to ___ the new mod - ern age! And

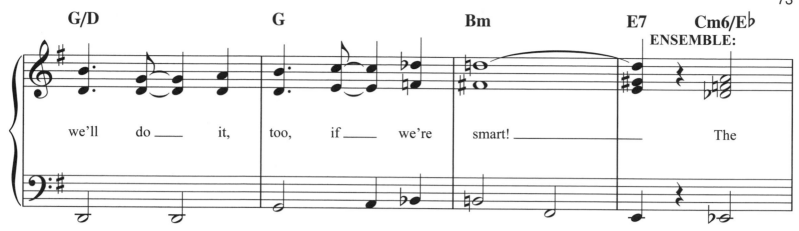

we'll do ___ it, too, if ___ we're smart! _____ The

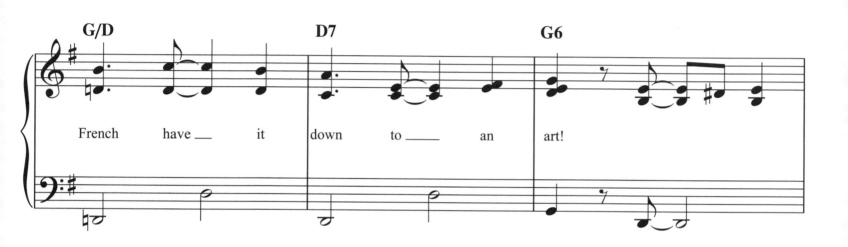

French have ___ it down to ___ an art!

Ev - 'ry - one's a

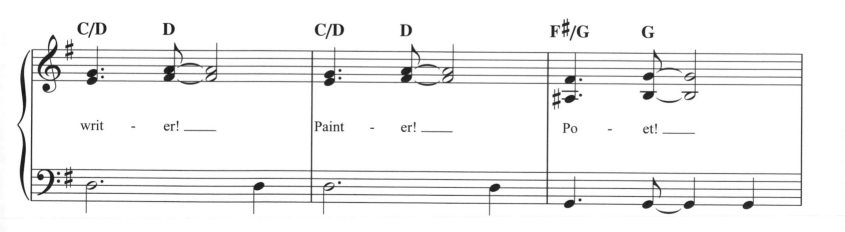

writ - er! ___ Paint - er! ___ Po - et! ___

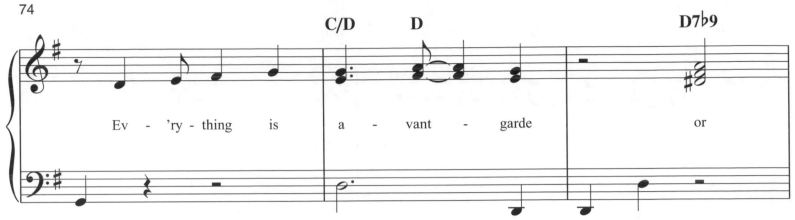

Ev - 'ry - thing is a - vant - garde or

chic! We'll be in the know be -

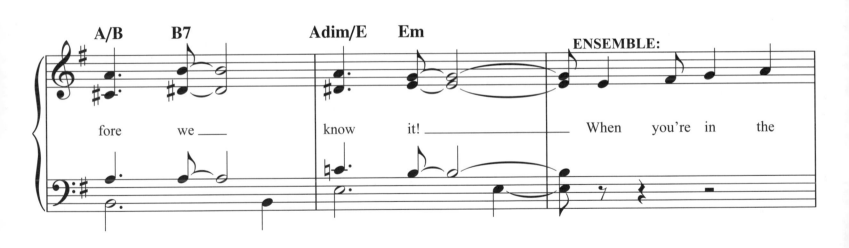

fore we ___ know it! ___ When you're in the

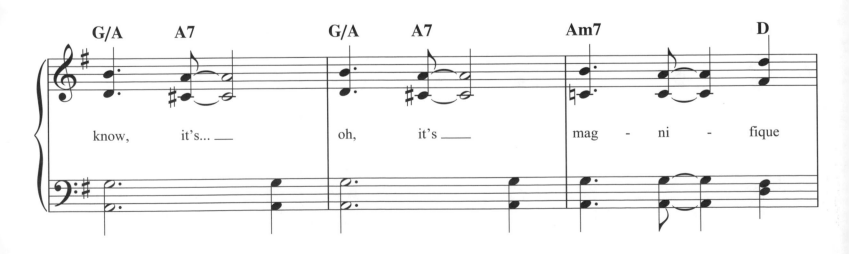

know, it's... ___ oh, it's ___ mag - ni - fique

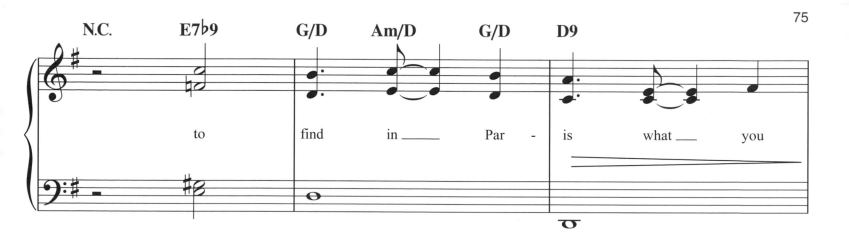

to find in _____ Par - is what ____ you

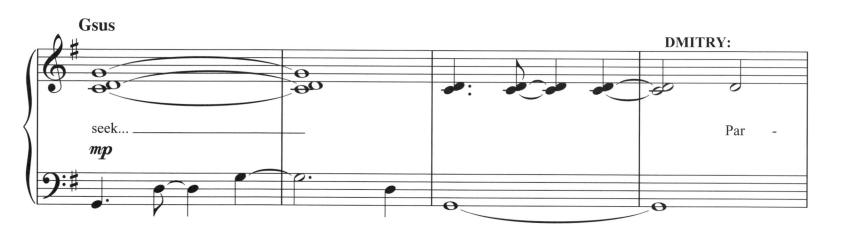

seek... _____ Par -

is holds the key to her fate. _____ We

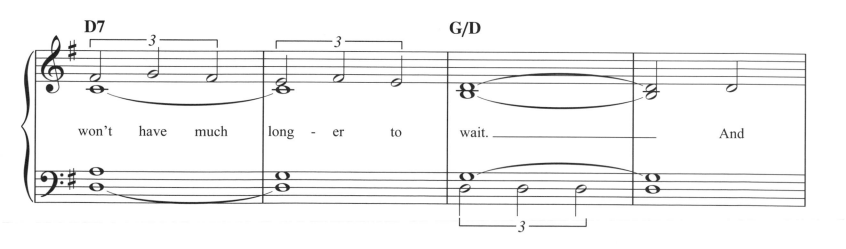

won't have much long - er to wait. _____ And

then, come what may, _____ we will each go our way... _____ I

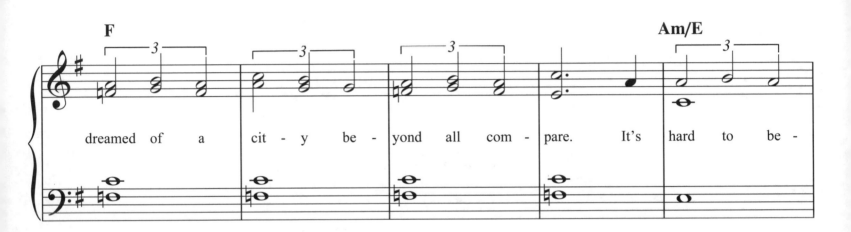

dreamed of a cit - y be - yond all com - pare. It's hard to be -

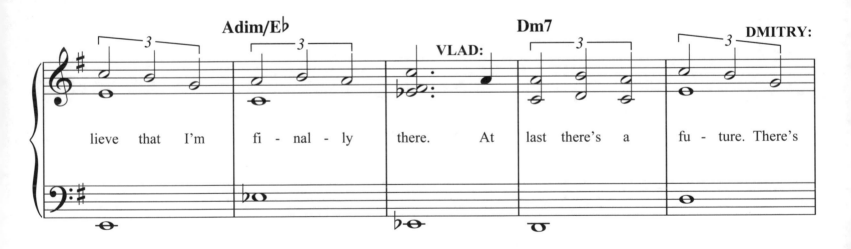

lieve that I'm fi - nal - ly there. At last there's a fu - ture. There's

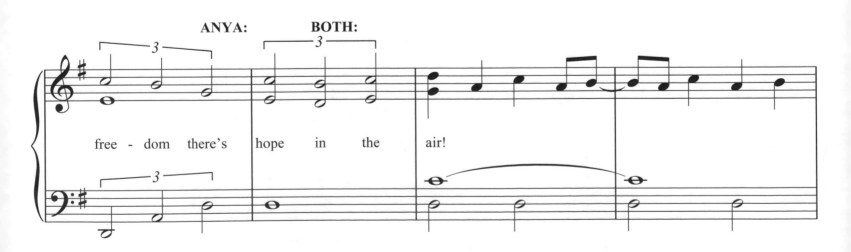

free - dom there's hope in the air!

ENSEMBLE:

Par -

is   holds ___ the   key   to ___   your   heart!   The

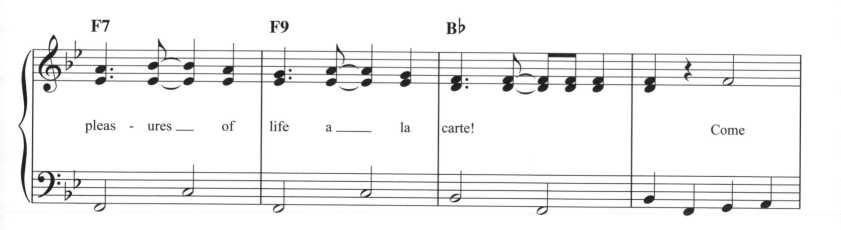

pleas - ures ___   of   life   a ___   la   carte!   Come

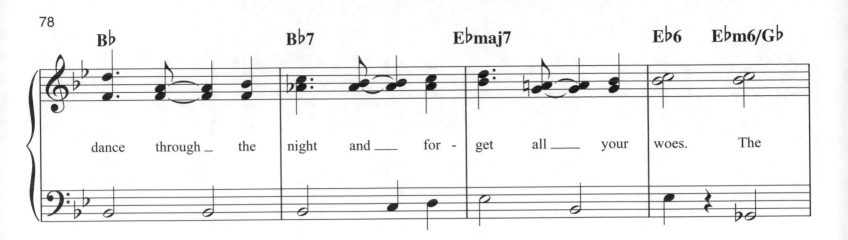

dance through __ the night and __ for - get all __ your woes. The

Ci - ty __ of Light! How __ it glit - ters __ and glows! And

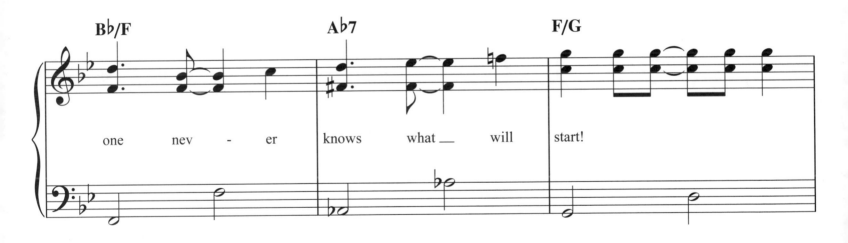

one nev - er knows what __ will start!

Par - is holds the

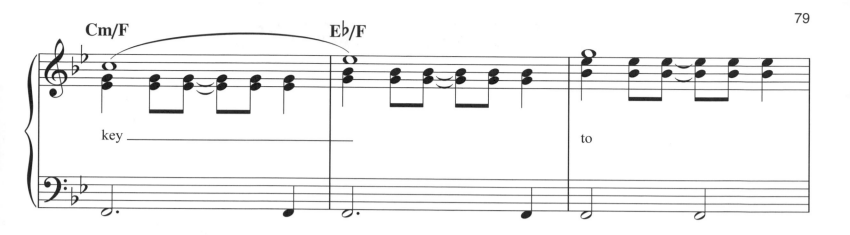

CROSSING A BRIDGE

Lyrics by LYNN AHRENS
Music by STEPHEN FLAHERTY

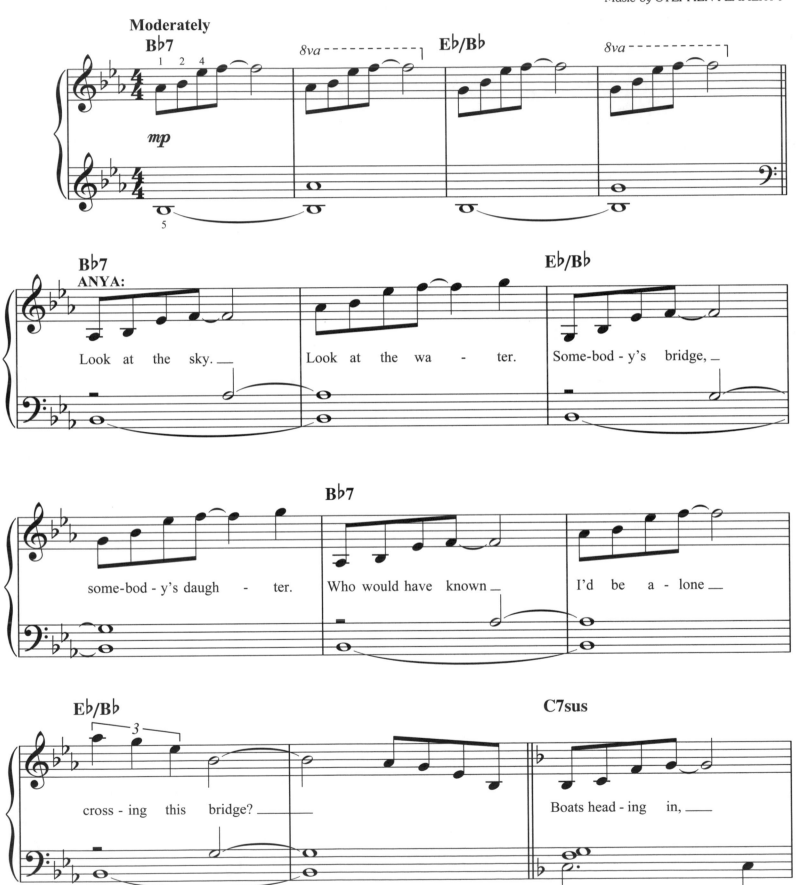

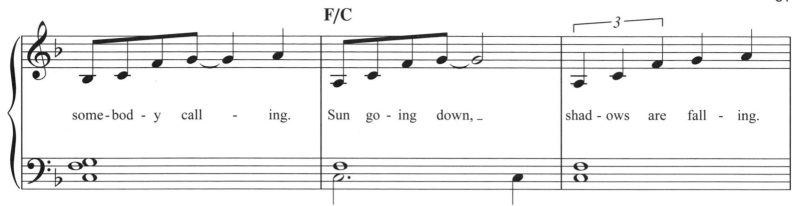

some-bod - y call - ing. Sun go - ing down, __ shad - ows are fall - ing.

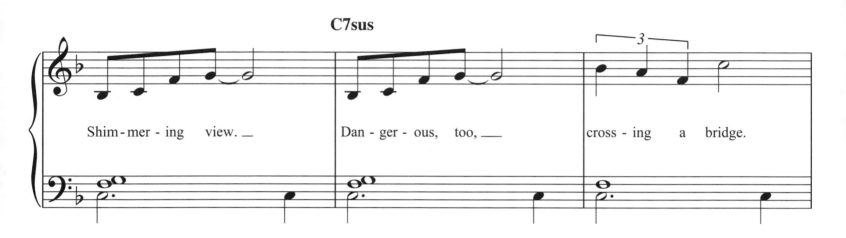

Shim - mer - ing view. __ Dan - ger - ous, too, __ cross - ing a bridge.

Half - way be - tween where I've been and

where I'm go - ing, __ in be - tween won - der - ing

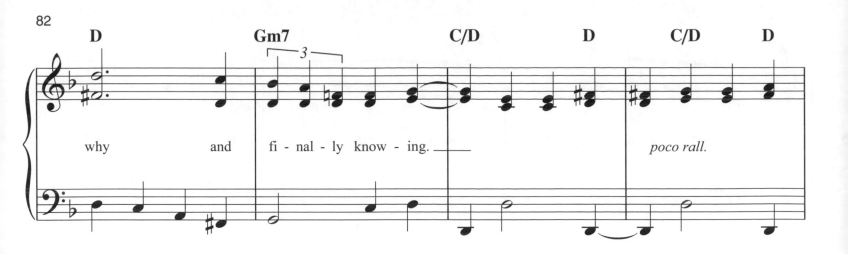

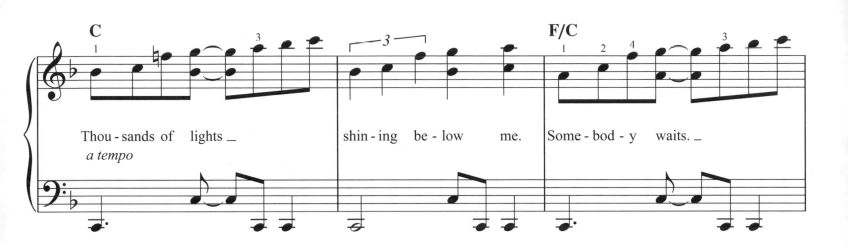

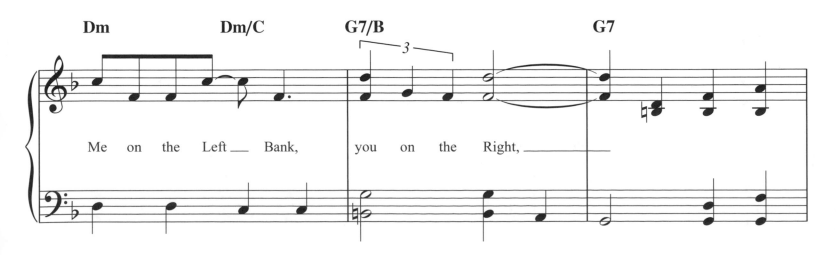

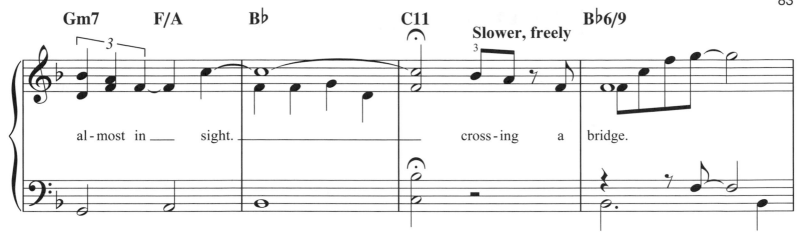

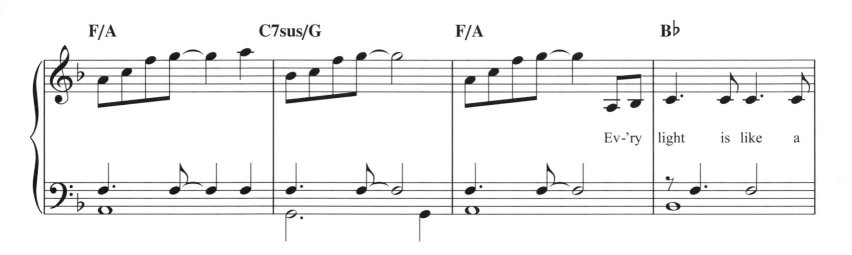

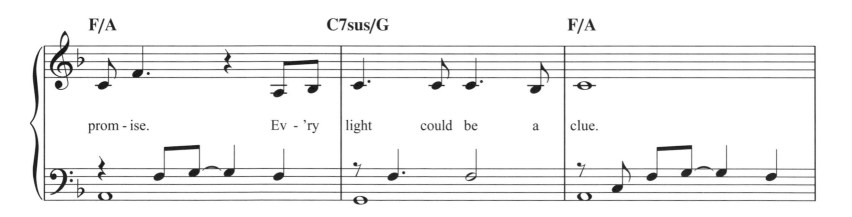

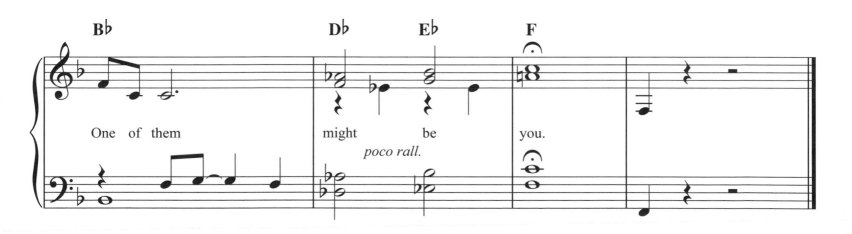

CLOSE THE DOOR

Lyrics by LYNN AHRENS
Music by STEPHEN FLAHERTY

Più mosso

where does sum - mer go? I will nev - er know. Sum - mer used to last

end - less - ly. Chil - dren all in white, run - ning down the sand to

me, _____ to me...

poco rit.

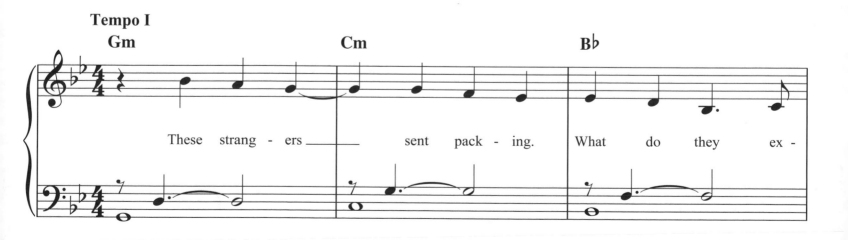

Tempo I

These strang - ers _____ sent pack - ing. What do they ex -

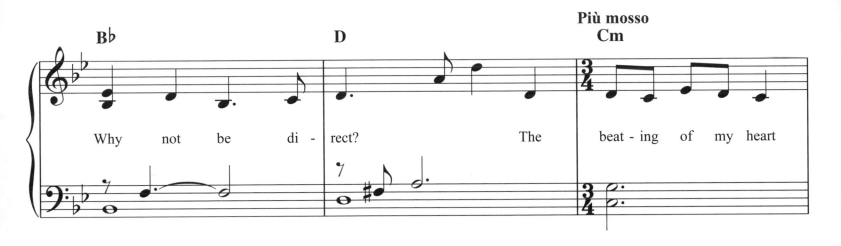

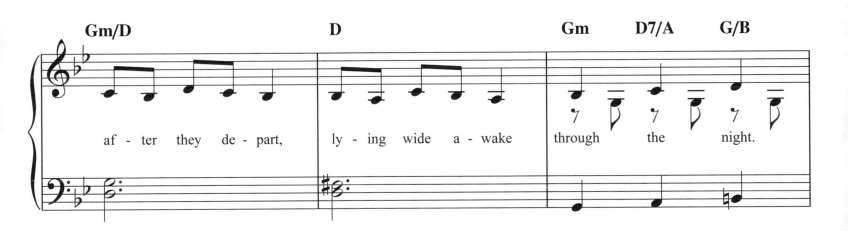

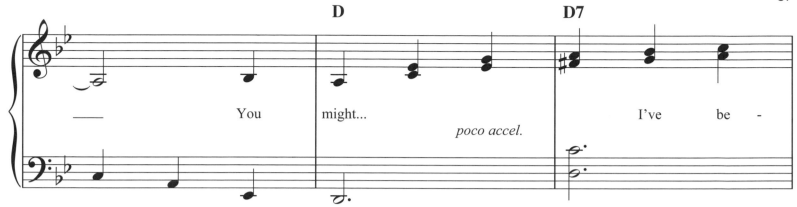

You might... I've be-

poco accel.

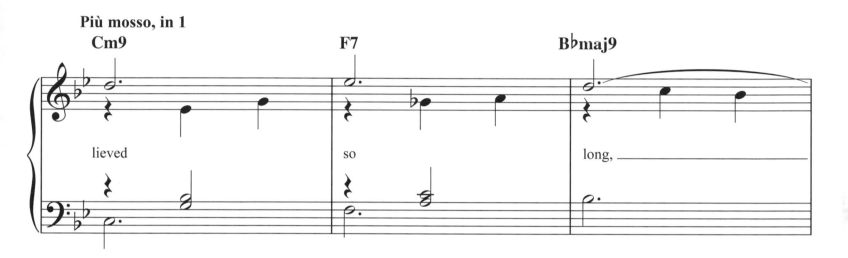

Più mosso, in 1

lieved so long,

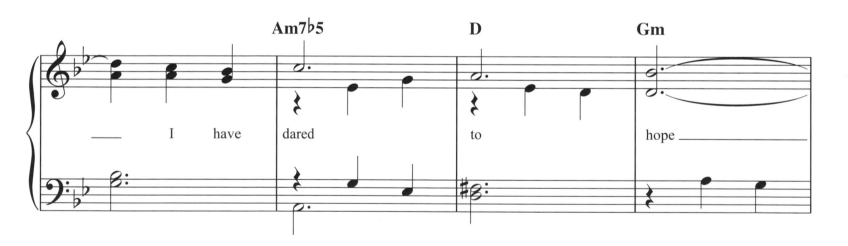

I have dared to hope

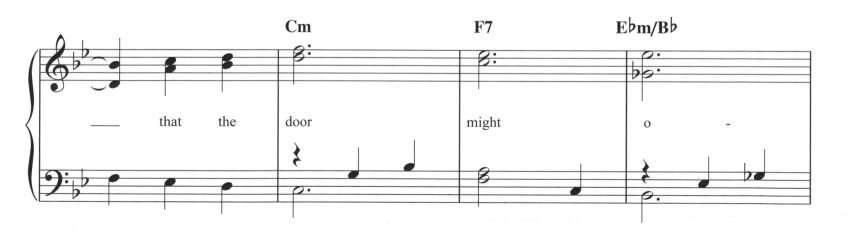

that the door might o -

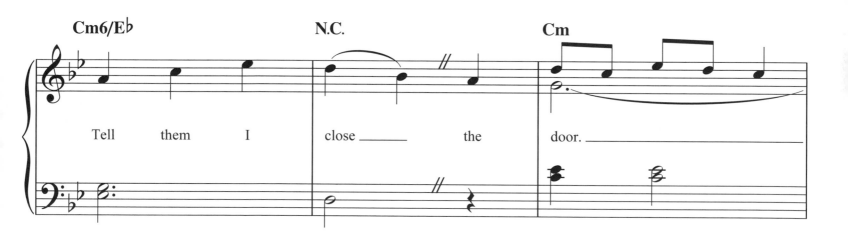

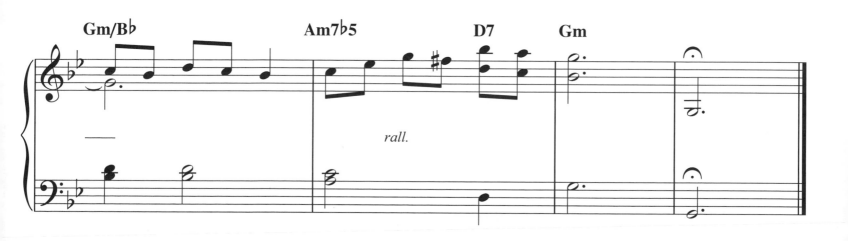

IN A CROWD OF THOUSANDS

Lyrics by LYNN AHRENS
Music by STEPHEN FLAHERTY

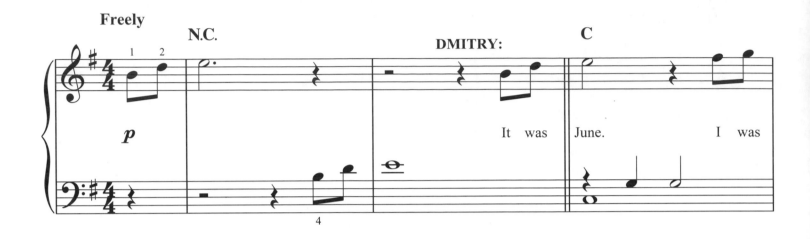

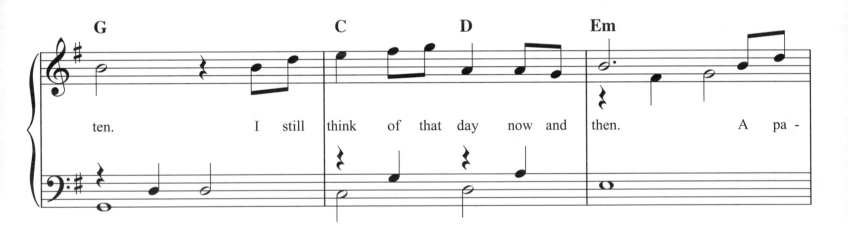

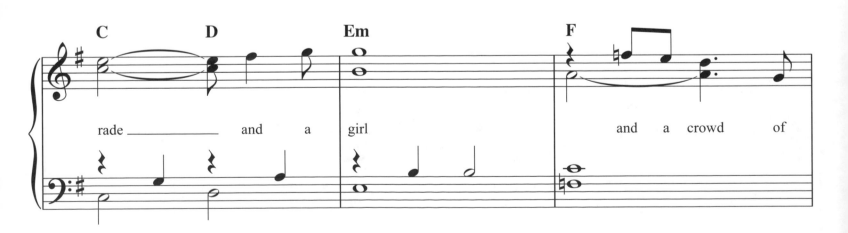

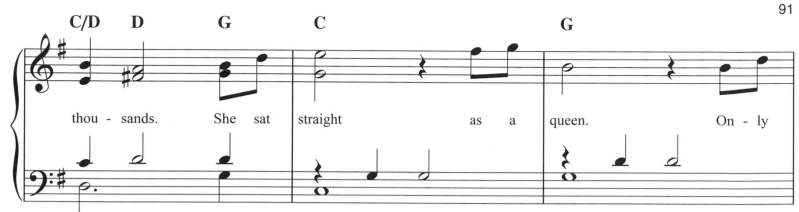

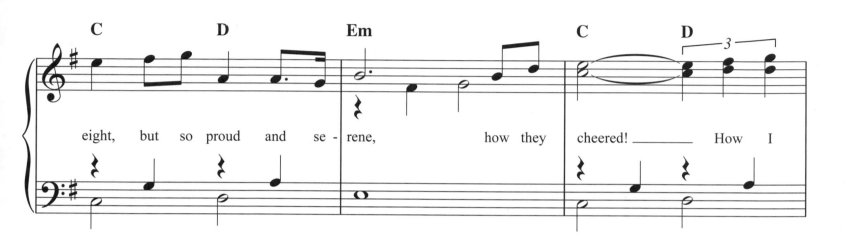

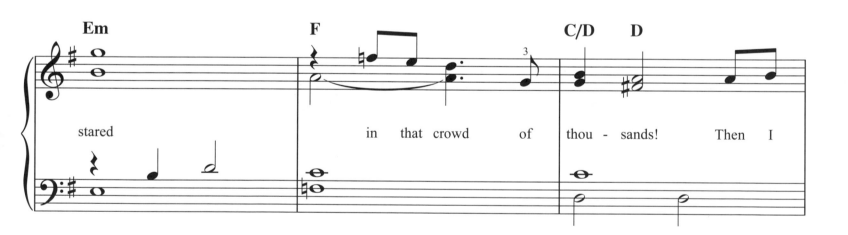

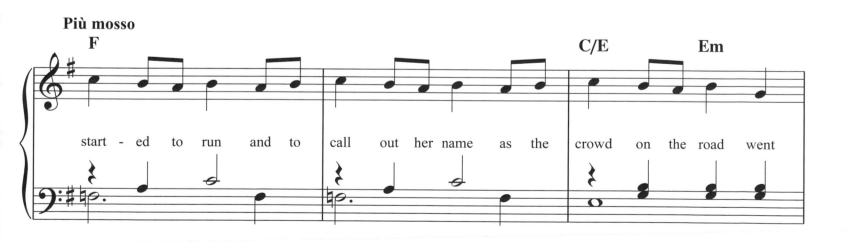

wild! I reached out with my hand and looked up and then she

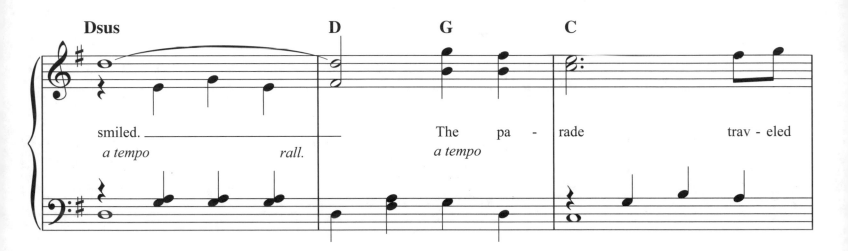

smiled. _____ The pa - rade trav - eled

a tempo *rall.* *a tempo*

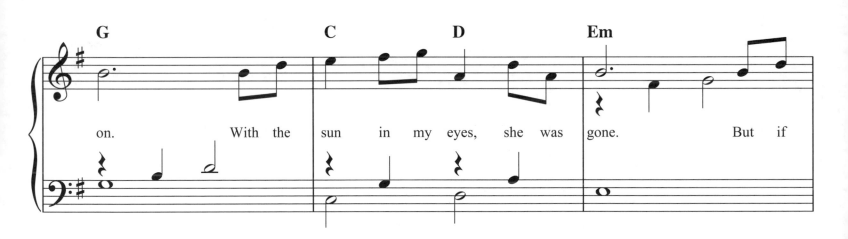

on. With the sun in my eyes, she was gone. But if

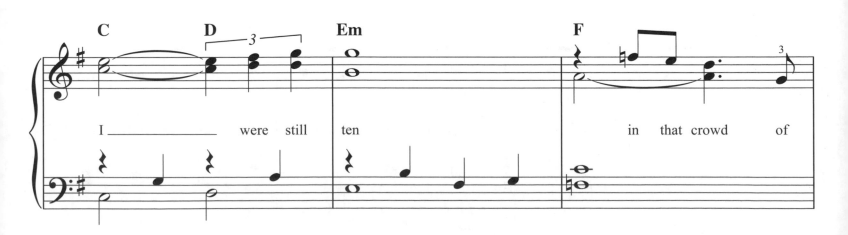

I _____ were still ten in that crowd of

Em ... **Cmaj7** ... **D**

thou - sands, I'd find her a -

Slightly relaxed

C ... **G/B** ... **C**

gain. *p*

ANYA: *You're making me feel I was there, too.*

DMITRY: *Maybe you were. Make it part of your story.*

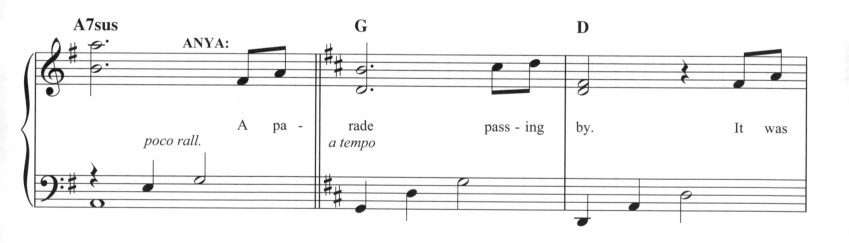

A7sus ... **G** ... **D**

poco rall.

ANYA:

A pa - *a tempo* rade pass - ing by. It was

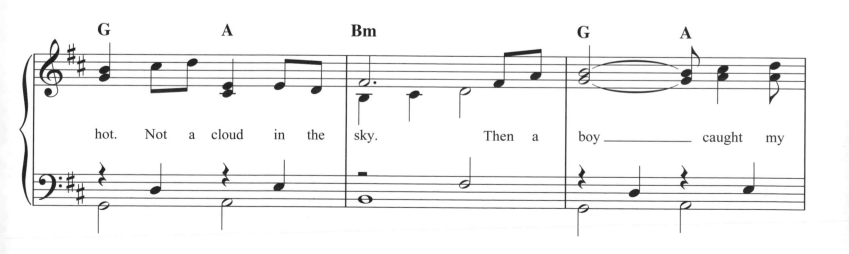

G ... **A** ... **Bm** ... **G** ... **A**

hot. Not a cloud in the sky. Then a boy _____ caught my

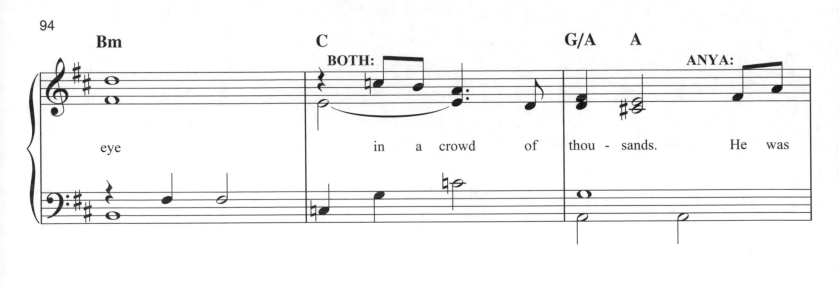

eye in a crowd of thou - sands. He was

thin. Not too clean. There were guards, but he dodged in be-

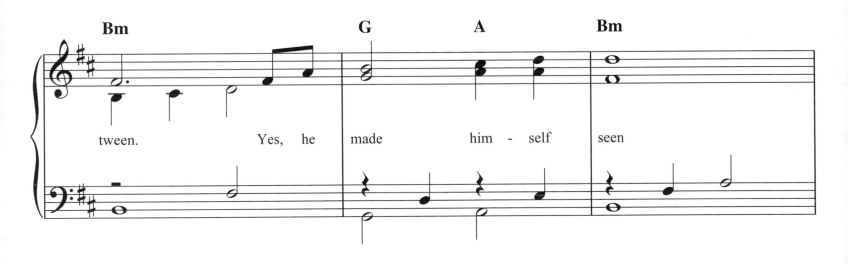

tween. Yes, he made him - self seen

in that crowd of thou - sands! Then he called out my name and he

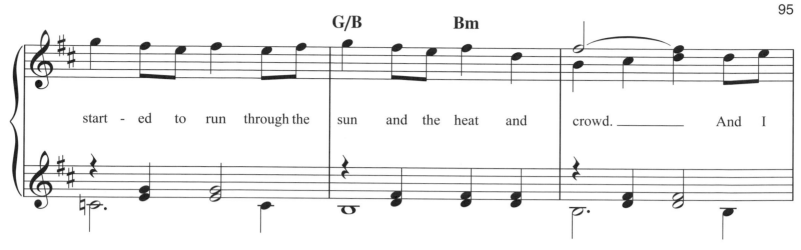

started to run through the sun and the heat and crowd. _____ And I

tried not to smile, but I smiled... _____ and then he
rall.

A bit slower

bowed. _____
p

DMITRY: *I didn't tell you that.*

ANYA: *You didn't have to, I remember.*

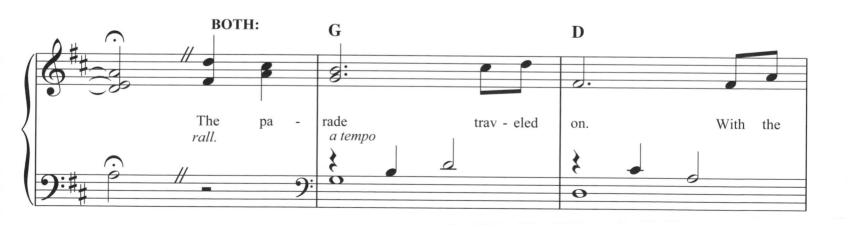

BOTH:

The pa - rade trav - eled on. With the
rall. *a tempo*

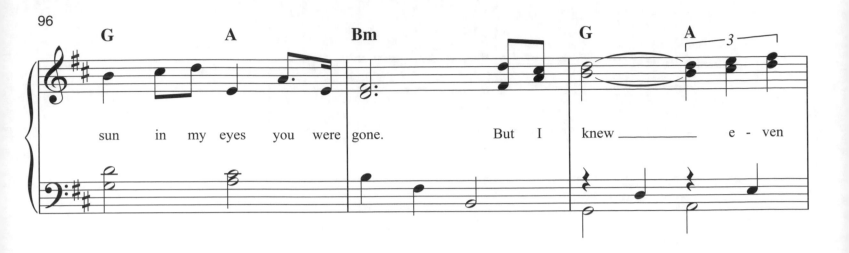

sun in my eyes you were gone. But I knew _____ e - ven

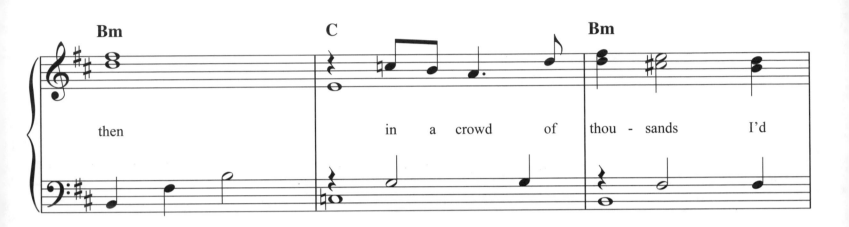

then in a crowd of thou - sands I'd

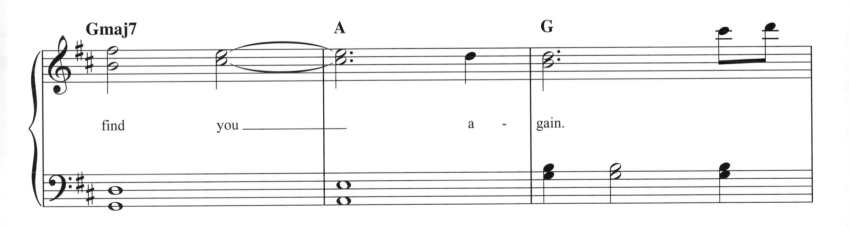

find you _____ a - gain.

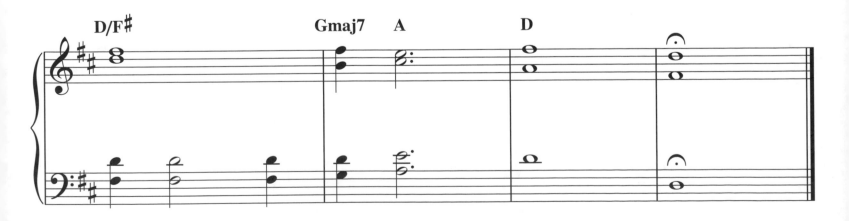

EVERYTHING TO WIN

Lyrics by LYNN AHRENS
Music by STEPHEN FLAHERTY

With movement and tension, in 2

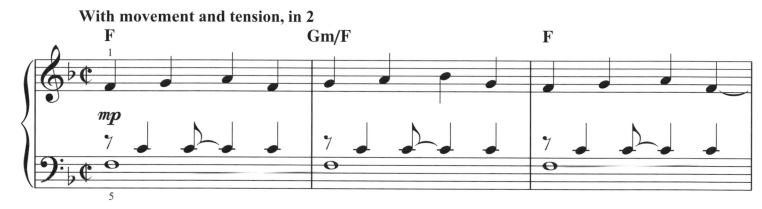

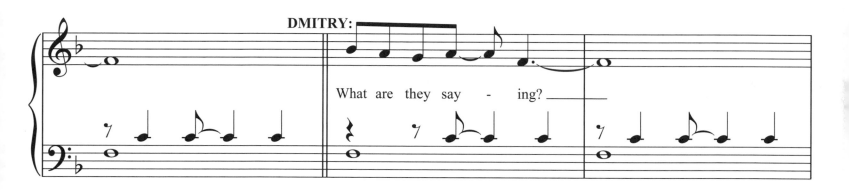

DMITRY: What are they say - ing? ____

Won - der how long ___ they'll be? Why should I wor - ry?

Wor - ry - ing's not ___ like me!

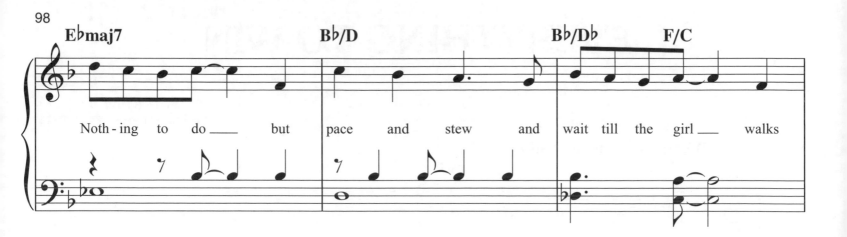

This could be bad, ___ but no! Let's as-sume ___ it's good.

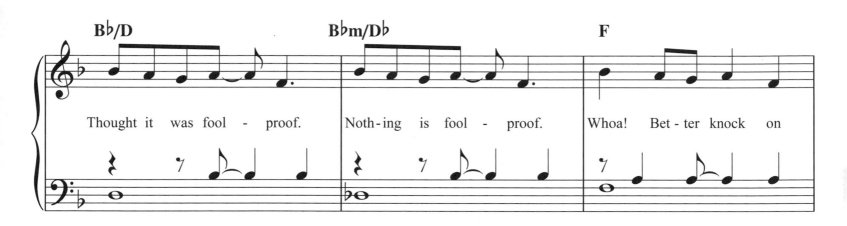

Thought it was fool - proof. Noth-ing is fool - proof. Whoa! Bet - ter knock on

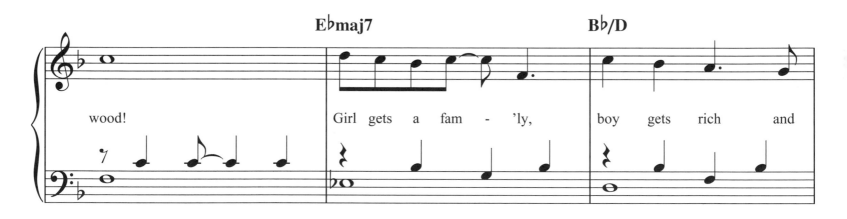

wood! Girl gets a fam - 'ly, boy gets rich and

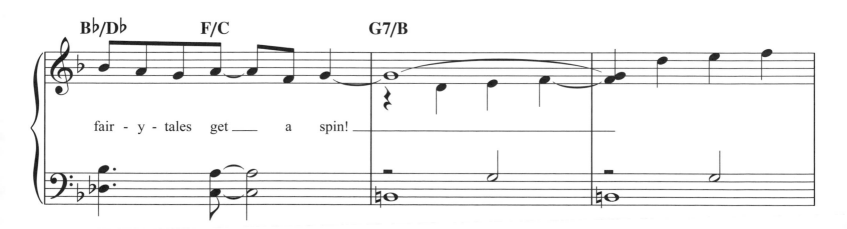

fair - y - tales get ___ a spin!

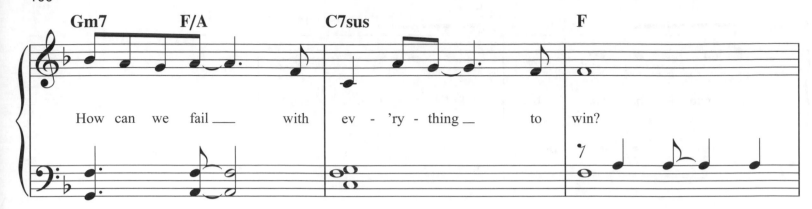

How can we fail ___ with ev - 'ry - thing ___ to win?

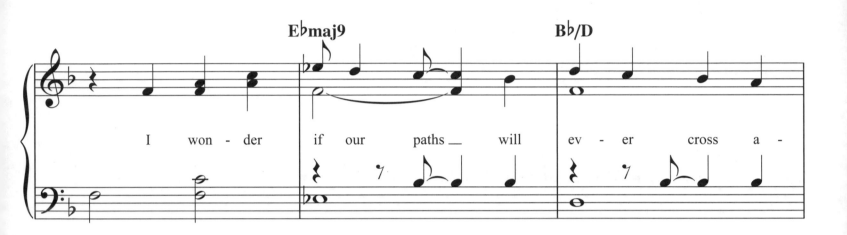

I won - der if our paths ___ will ev - er cross a -

gain the way they did when you ___ were

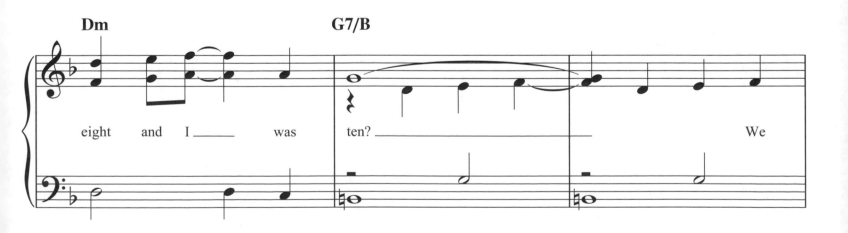

eight and I ___ was ten? ___ We

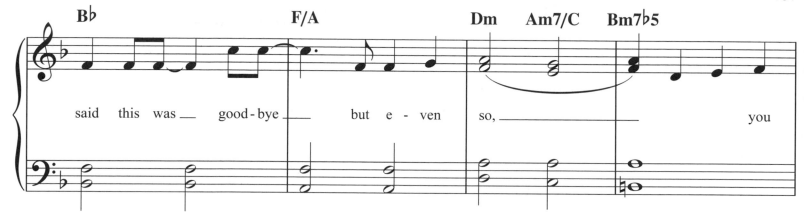

said this was good-bye but e - ven so, you

nev - er know, you nev - er know.

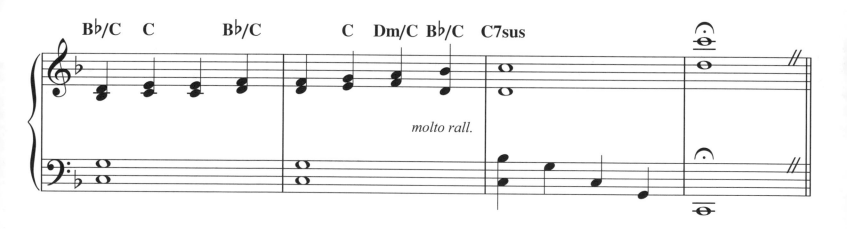

molto rall.

Simply (rubato)

I should be glad that we're break-ing free but noth-ing is what it was.

I did - n't know __ she mat - tered to me, __ but

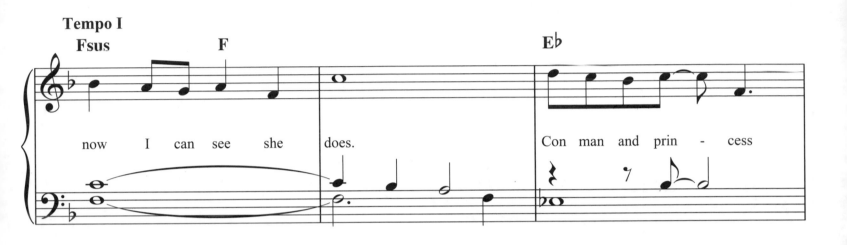

Tempo I

now I can see she does.

Con man and prin - cess

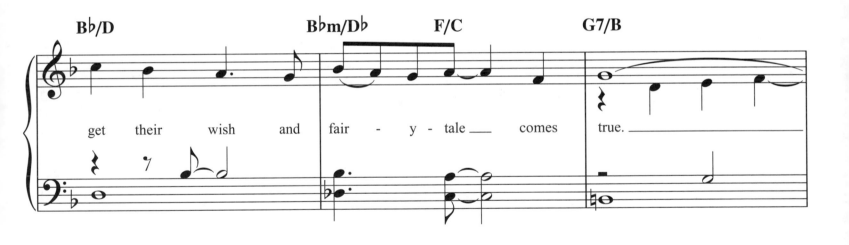

get their wish and fair - y - tale __ comes true. __

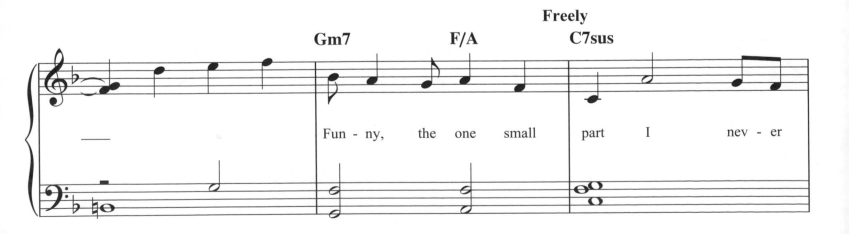

Fun - ny, the one small part I nev - er

More deliberately, in 4

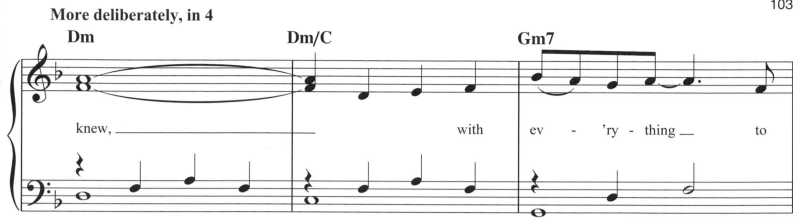

knew, _____ with ev - 'ry - thing _____ to

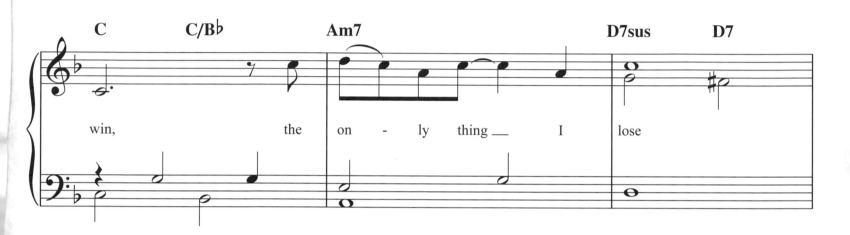

win, the on - ly thing _____ I lose

poco rit. is you. _____ *a tempo*

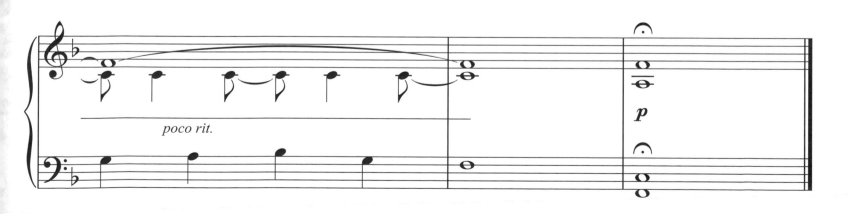

poco rit. *p*